FIRESTONE

PARK

POLICING SOUTH CENTRAL LOS ANGELES

By

JERRY BOYD, M.S.

CHIEF OF POLICE, RETIRED

DEDICATION

This book is dedicated to Los Angeles County Sheriff's Sergeant Tommy Thompson and Deputy Frank Oakden. May both rest in peace. They were my mentors during my teen years when I served as a Disaster Communications Volunteer with the Sheriff's Department. They recruited me to become a member of the Department. Nearly eight years with LASD were followed by another thirty-seven years in public safety – a great professional career thanks in large part to Tommy and Frank.

ACKNOWLEDGMENTS

I would like to acknowledge all who worked at Firestone Station over the years, and in particular those who were there during the period 1968-1971 and 1974, when it was my honor to work with them. Many of them were partners in the stories told in this book. Without the good partners I was privileged to work with, I might not have survived to tell these stories or write this book.

My first wife, Patty, was my partner and supporter during and after my time at Firestone. My career, in many respects, became what it was because of her. May she rest in peace.

I also want to thank my wife, Jay, and my daughter, Ruthie, for encouraging me to write this book. It may be that they tired of hearing the "war stories" and wanted them in book form so they could pick it up and read at their convenience rather than listen to me ramble on.

I want to thank Jay as well for the editing and proof work she did on the book. That was a huge workload and she did it well.

About The Author

Jerry Boyd was born and raised in Los Angeles County and at the age of 18 began service as a Technical Reserve in Disaster Communications with the Los Angeles County Sheriff's Department (LASD) in southern California. In 1968, he began his full time career with LASD as a Deputy Sheriff. Upon graduation from the training academy, Jerry was transferred to patrol at Firestone Station. It was that initial assignment that provides the "fodder" for many of the stories in this book. After a stint working Headquarters Detectives, Jerry was promoted to Sergeant in 1972, and once again found himself working the mean streets of south-central Los Angeles.

In 1975, the author left LASD to join the newly formed Irvine, California, Police Department as a Lieutenant. He served as a Patrol Area Commander and created the Department's Special Weapons and Tactics (SWAT) Team. He was promoted to Captain in 1978, and commanded Operations Division until he left to become Chief of Police in Coronado, California in 1981. After serving in Coronado for ten years, he completed his full time law enforcement career with five years as Chief of Police in Martinez, California. Jerry has also served in other communities as chief of a Volunteer Fire/Rescue Department, Emergency Management Director, as well as a director of a 9-1-1 Dispatch Center from 2003 until the present time.

Jerry has served as an instructor at numerous law enforcement training academies, colleges, universities, and law schools. He holds a Master of Science degree in Criminal Justice Administration from California State University at Long Beach. He is the author of six previously published books on public safety topics. Jerry writes the "From the Chief" column in each issue of *AmericanCop* magazine.

Email Jerry at exlasd@msn.com

DISCLAIMER

I'm not like Rush Limbaugh. While every story contained in this book is true, they are all based upon memory. Since many of these incidents occurred 40 plus years ago, that may not result in the 99.6% accuracy that Rush claims....but they are close. I hope you enjoy them.

FOREWORD

With over 300 million Americans and approximately only 1 million law enforcement officers – encompassing local city, county, state, and federal agencies – it is safe to say that the majority of American citizens have never had a "personal encounter" with a law enforcement officer. Those who have had that "personal experience" fall into one of the following categories: Individuals who break the law and/or commit the crime (yes, that even includes traffic tickets); individuals who are the victims of a crime; individuals who witness a crime; those who are victims of an accident (such as a car accident or natural disaster of some type); and those individuals who have friends or family members in law enforcement.

There are many authors in the Mystery/Crime/Suspense genre – my personal favorite reading subject – and many writers in the movie and television industries who develop the stories we see almost every time we turn on the television. Almost all of these productions have a technical advisor who is a former or retired cop. However, many of these authors and writers never worked as a "cop". They may have tried to get some idea of what a cop goes through by going as a "ride-along" – a program offered by some law enforcement agencies – where they ride in a patrol car with actual police officers. Then there are those who were cops, such as the highly successful author, Joseph Wambaugh, for example, who wrote his stories based on his experiences as a Los Angeles police officer.

Many years ago, one of the first statements my college English/Creative Writing professor said during her introduction to the class was, "If you want to write, write about what you know. It is much easier. If you try to write about something you don't know, you will have a much more difficult time."

Creative imagination can only take a writer so far, and that is sometimes exaggerated to an extent that would result in unreal description and expectation. A good example is in writing war stories. Many of the books about war and combat are written by those who were there and experienced the rigors, atrocities, horrors, and emotions of war – like seeing a young man you know, who at one moment is right there beside you, and in a blink of an eye, you see that person's head explode from a sniper's bullet. These are stories that can only be told by someone who has done it.

Every day in police work, somewhere in the country, a police officer faces a situation wherein he has only a split-second to make a decision that could result in death of either himself or another, if the wrong decision were to be made.

This book is an outstanding example of writing about what you know. Jerry illustrates that cops are human. Throughout the book, he uses his writing abilities to take you, the reader, to that special place where you feel as if you are right there alongside him.

Jerry starts out back in 1968 – an era where cops on the street faced the same dangers as they do today. However, there were some differences.

In those days, the deputies carried a county-issued Smith & Wesson Model 15 .38 caliber 4" barrel revolver that held 6 bullets. It was carried in a "swivel" holster on their "Sam Browne" gun belt. Also on the belt was what was called a "dump pouch" for carrying 12 rounds of extra ammunition. It consisted of two separate pouches, each for holding 6 rounds of .38 caliber ammunition. The pouches were closed by a flap with a snap on the bottom. When extra rounds were needed, the deputy would unsnap a pouch and the bullets would fall into his hand – or so it says in the fine print. Most of the time, at least one round would fall to the ground. Another item on the belt was the handcuff case that held one pair of handcuffs. Then, the last piece on the belt was a baton ring: a metal ring attached to a small leather strap. The baton had a rubber stopper around it to prevent it from falling through the ring. The Sam Browne Belt was held in place by the use of four "keeper" straps that would wrap around behind the deputy's uniform belt and come around and snap together on the outside of the Sam Browne Belt. There were two additional pockets on the rear of the uniform trousers designed to hold a flashlight and a "sap" (a leather-covered piece of metal with a handgrip). The deputy's field note book was sized specifically to fit in one of the rear trouser pockets.

Deputies carried items such as extra flashlight batteries, ammunition, report forms, pencils, pens, paper clips, extra gloves, penal code books, traffic citation books, electrical tape, duct tape, the indispensable "Thomas Guide" map book, and other "personal items" as desired, in a regular office-supply type metal file folder box.

Individual Body Armor had not come into existence yet.

Deputies would stand inspection prior to the beginning of the shift by the watch sergeant. Attention was given to personal and uniform appearance. This included the proper wearing of the "Sam Browne". Appearance was a high priority for the Sheriff, Peter J. Pitchess.

There were no portable individual communication radios, no cell/camera phones, no "tasers", collapsible batons, first aid packets, rubber glove containers.

There were no computers in the radio cars, or in the station. All reports were done by hand, in pencil and turned into the watch sergeant prior to the end of shift.

From the beginning, where Jerry writes about his first three months working at the Men's Central Jail, one of the main facilities in the nation's largest jail system, while he is waiting to attend the academy to learn how to be a deputy sheriff, he faces some situations that could result in serious injury to himself and others.

These incidents do not make the nightly news nor do they appear in the daily paper. These could not be imagined by the average citizen. When he is finally transferred to the academy, he encounters more situations that, again, are not publicized. The Los Angeles County Sheriff's Academy was known for stressing the students – known as cadets – to the point where some would voluntarily resign, some in tears. They figured that if you couldn't take being yelled at constantly, and either broke down or lost your temper, you wouldn't be able to handle yourself when on patrol in the streets. Jerry explains how the department decided to compare two different methods of the training: stress and non-stress. Again, the mental and physical limits of the cadets were put to the test.

Upon graduation from the academy, Jerry takes you with him as he reports in to Firestone Station for his assignment to Patrol Division. From being a "trainee" assigned to a Training Officer (T.O.), who was a very experienced deputy, to his becoming a regular patrol deputy who dislikes working a traffic car, yet gets various assignments to working traffic, and becomes a T.O. himself, is, again, written in such a way so that you feel you are in the car with him.

Throughout the book there are stories that bring forth emotions such as sadness and tragedy, humor and joy, highs and lows, various personalities, and situations, that only a cop can tell. Jerry's curriculum vitae shows that he is definitely one who has "Been there, done that, got the T-shirt."

I know. I spent my first 10 years (1962-1972) of a 21-year law enforcement career as a Los Angeles County Deputy Sheriff. I went through a 20-week, highly stress-motivated period known as the Los Angeles County Sheriff's Academy. I spent almost two years working the jail before I transferred to Firestone Station – one week before the start of the 1965 Watts Riots. I thoroughly experienced all of those emotions we each possess, and life-threatening situations which occurred during my 6-years in Patrol Division.

For those of you who "wear the badge", whether you are on a large department or a small department, you will enjoy this book. For those of you not in the law enforcement community, this book gives you an insight as to what it was like – and still is – to police one of the most dangerous and active crime areas in the nation. It is a great and enjoyable read.

Harry D. Penny, Jr.

Author of:

- *BEHIND THE BADGE: The Funny Side of the "Thin Blue Line"*
- *NAVY CORPSMAN: I'm the One Called "Doc"* (Due for release Spring of 2012)

Chapter I:

Introduction

I was born in Los Angeles County not long after the end of World War II. My parents, like many others, had migrated to California from the Midwest during the war. My dad worked in the defense industry building aircraft for Lockheed. After the war ended, my father became employed as a maintenance superintendent for a very large company which owned hundreds of apartments in the LA area. Many of those apartments, like the large complex where we lived, were not in the very best areas of the city.

My schooling, from first grade through high school, was in the Catholic school system. I attended Resurrection Elementary and Bishop Mora Salesian High School. Both were situated in Boyle Heights just east of downtown Los Angeles, on the fringe of what is known as East Los Angeles. While the very large apartment complex we lived in was relatively crime-free, the same could not be said of the general neighborhood, particularly the areas I had to walk through going to and from school. While LA did not have the hundreds of gangs it does today, within a mile of my home there were two large and historic gangs. "White Fence" was predominantly black and named for the white fence that surrounded the public housing project where most of the members of that gang lived. "Barrio Nuevo" was the Mexican gang which occupied most of the rest of Boyle Heights "turf" and, indeed, much of East Los Angeles.

The schools I attended were diverse in ethnic makeup. My four Anglo friends and I were the definite minority in high school. My graduating class was predominantly Mexican with a large number of blacks, Japanese, and even some Chinese thrown into the mix. I would comment that the Hispanics of that day were not illegal aliens as so many in that area today are. Their parents came here legally – many to work in agriculture (yes, much of southern California was still agricultural back then, not wall-to-wall concrete as it is today).

Living in that neighborhood taught me several things. One, I learned a great deal of Spanish even before taking that language in school. That later served me well as a member of the Los Angeles County Sheriff's Department (LASD) and for that matter still serves me well today. Two, I learned to relate to people of many ethnic backgrounds without developing any particular prejudices. My prejudices were not against blacks or Mexicans because of their ethnicity. Any blacks or Hispanics I came to dislike were those in the gangs because they frequently targeted those few of us "Anglos" who dared walk through their turf as we went about our business.

That reality – being the target of gangs – was not a pleasant one. More than once I had a knife pulled on me and my hard earned paper route money stolen at knifepoint. Plus, there were a few times I got beat up pretty badly. That led to a couple of other "learning points": one, I learned how to avoid conflicts if at all possible; and two, I learned how to defend myself without resorting to deadly weapons. I also learned that the "thin blue line" of law enforcement was the only thing that kept the criminal element from totally victimizing the law abiding.

From a fairly early age I had pretty much decided I wanted to be a cop. Truth be known, I envisioned myself as a member of the Los Angeles Police Department (LAPD) because they, not the Sheriff, policed the area in which I lived. Plus, the security guard that worked for our apartment complex was a retired LAPD officer, and most of the TV cop shows of the day (*Dragnet* comes to mind, among others) featured LAPD as well.

My parents were always very supportive of what I chose to do. I played basketball in high school, and they never missed a game. Through a friend I became interested in amateur ("ham") radio and my dad, who was already very adept at things electronic, helped me build my first radio station after I obtained my FCC license. What they did not willingly support was my desire to become a cop.

PREPARING FOR LAW ENFORCEMENT

When I graduated from high school, I was admitted, on a borderline high school academic record, to a very prestigious (and expensive) college. Much to my shock, Loyola University of Los Angeles admitted me as a freshman, but on a probationary status. I had one semester to prove I could hack it academically. Coincidently I had saved just enough money to pay tuition, books, and other expenses for one semester.

Loyola didn't have a "criminal justice" program to major in, so I thought the next best thing that would help me eventually be a good cop was a combination of psychology, sociology, and political science. I also thought it was time to buckle down and study since I had probation hanging over my head. Of course, I had no idea how I'd pay for it if they did decide to let me stay beyond semester one.

At the end of my first semester, I had a 4.0 average. The University, which in spite of my later philosophical differences with it over whether it is really "Catholic", made my college education possible, and for that I thank them. For the remainder of my freshman year, I had all of my expenses paid for by the University on a "work study scholarship". I was assigned to work several hours a day in the library after my classes; in exchange, my tuition and books were free. At the end of my freshman year, I still had a 4.0 grade point average, and maintained that in my major for all four years of college. As a result of my academic performance, I wound up with a full-ride scholarship just like the cool athletes got! Not a bad deal at all.

While at Loyola, I met my future bride, Patty. We married several weeks before I graduated, and we had three sons, one of whom has been in law enforcement for 23 years. Patty died on our 18th wedding anniversary, but was my loyal supporter and confidante during the most difficult times of my law enforcement career.

In spite of my parents and others discouraging me from entering law enforcement after college, I did just that. But it wasn't LAPD. Through my "hobby" of ham radio, I had begun serving as a Disaster Communications Technical Reserve with LASD as soon as I had turned 18. The coordinators of that program, Sergeant Tommy Thompson and Deputy Frank Oakden, got me to thinking a tan and green uniform was preferable to LAPD's all blue. So not long after college and marriage, I joined LASD and never turned back. As of this writing, I have been in public safety, predominantly law enforcement, for over forty-five years. If I said I've enjoyed every minute of it, I'd be lying. Some things you encounter on the streets as a cop you simply can't enjoy. But I will say if I had to do it all over again, I wouldn't hesitate for a micro second.

CHAPTER II:

LA COUNTY MEN'S CENTRAL JAIL

I was hired by LASD following an extensive testing process. LASD was on a hiring binge at the time and brought new deputies on several months before the start of the training academy itself. In that interim period, new deputies were assigned "off the street" usually to one of the Department's several jail facilities. LASD was and is the world's largest Sheriff's Department and runs a jail system larger than the statewide prison system in most states.

I was assigned, pre-academy, to Men's Central Jail (MCJ). At the time, it was a massive concrete and steel complex just north of downtown LA not far from City Hall, Chinatown, and the city's largest train station. It housed thousands of inmates ranging from common drunks doing a couple of days in the tank to murderers awaiting trial or back from state prison on appeal. The "heavy weight" serious offenders were housed in a special "high power" module. They ranged from cop killers to Charles Manson and just about every serious offender in between.

It was the "high power" module to which I was assigned during most of the three months I spent working the jail before the start of the academy. It was that three months which convinced me that, if at all possible, I did *not* want to spend much time on jail duty if I survived the academy.

Uh-Oh

I'd like to say my stint at MCJ was uneventful. That, however, would be untrue. As but one example of how "Murphy" did his best to end my career early, I offer this. One evening, the "high powers" were being fed dinner in the chow hall, and I was assigned inside that large room with three other deputies. Our task was to insure that everyone stayed "mellow". Now you have to understand that on their best day some of the inmates in that room, who were heavily sedated due to mental "issues", were incapable of being mellow. I was new and nobody had bothered to explain to me that the kinder, more gentle approach was always the first choice when dealing with those folks.

That particular evening, one of the high powers, who I happened to know was one of the cop killers made famous in Joe Wambaugh's book, *The Onion Field,* "flipped out" as I was walking by his table. Actually, he flipped his dinner tray at me, and my clean, well-pressed uniform was now adorned with gravy and mashed potatoes, among other things.

Using an arm bar (which I hadn't been officially taught but did know how to apply), I forced the inmate back down onto the bench where he was supposed to sit. I wasn't brutal, but I wasn't gentle either. And I most certainly didn't say "pretty please".

Well, the place came unglued! The senior deputy on duty in the chow hall had to request immediate assistance from elsewhere in the jail. Inmates were assaulting deputies and each other. It took more than a few minutes and more than a few deputies to get it calmed down. The Sergeant had some "advice" to give me after it was all over.

Several years later, a deputy who was in that room transferred to Firestone Station where I was stationed by then. He shared with me that I came very close to getting fired that night. Had that occurred, my career would not have happened, nor would you be reading this book.

Chapter III:

The Academy

After almost three months of jail duty at MCJ, a transfer list teletype (today it would be email) came out assigning us "off-the-streeters" to an academy class. I was assigned to Class 127 and, strangely, was directed to report not to the Sheriff's Training Academy in East Los Angeles, but to the U S Marine Corps Reserve Armory in Chavez Ravine. That would be just down the road from Dodger Stadium, and not too much farther than that from the LAPD Academy. I, and others from MCJ assigned to Class 127, wondered what was up. We'd soon find out.

An Experiment

It seems that the Department's Assistant Sheriff, a well-known ivory-tower-thinker-about-town, and not much of a cop, had conceived a study. My classmates and I were going to be guinea pigs in that study, as if just surviving the 13 week academy was not difficult enough.

The Assistant Sheriff, whom I again emphasize was more of an academician than a cop, thought that with a "less military" type of academy the deputies produced would be "less prone to violent encounters", more "sensitive" and more "understanding" than their stress-trained counterparts. He was "politically correct" long before anyone ever knew what political correctness was.

Class 126 was assigned to the regular academy facility. It was to be the normal stress-based (physical and mental) academy. It would have 33 cadets assigned at the start, and it, too, would last 13 weeks. My class, 127, had 33 cadets assigned as well.

Now I don't want to say that the comparison study was flawed from the start, but consider this: Class126 met at the academy "campus", and the two drill instructors (DI's) assigned to the class were ex-Army. It was to be a stress class. Class 127, my class, met in a *US Marine Corps Armory* which was staffed *by US Marines*. Not to badmouth the Army, but there is only one kind of Marine, and they don't do non-stress. And the DI's assigned to our class were both former Marines. How they expected our class to be "non-stress" given our DI's and our environment is beyond me. Seriously – and on graduation day our DI's confirmed this – the only difference between class 126 and 127 was that their DI's yelled. Ours whispered in our ears – but they whispered the same derogatory comments and the same threats as their counterparts. I guess "more quiet" is the difference between stress and non-stress.

At the time I went through the academy, I was one of very few cops to have a BA degree. Frankly, I was not at all worried about the academic part of the academy. I wasn't worried about firearms qualification either, as I had done some shooting in the past. Even though I had been working out for six months prior to the academy starting and was in pretty good shape, the physical fitness part (which included defensive tactics) had me a bit nervous.

Mistake Number One

On day one of the academy, our DI's informed us that that afternoon we would have our first physical training (PT) evaluation. Dummy here made a huge mistake. I went "balls to the wall" and did the maximum number of push-ups, sit-ups, and pull-ups I was capable of. I also ran a 6-minute timed mile. I *am not* a 6-minute mile guy, but adrenaline can make the body do heroic things.

The next day, we had individual PT assessments with a DI. My DI said, "You're an animal. We really want to see how you improve over the next 13 weeks." I about died. I might make a few improvements, but I doubted I'd ever again run a 6-minute mile. And you know what? In the over 24,000 miles I have run since then (I was addicted to running 10K's, half-marathons, and marathons for over 13 years), I have never even come close.

The next 13 weeks were PT hell for me. During runs the DI's would yell, and they generally yelled at me. They accused me of "dogging it" on our usual 5-mile "jaunts through the park" because, as front "road guard", I often got run over by the rest of the class. They had started to fun faster, and I was already maxed out.

One of the things that got my attention in the first week of the Academy was the staff telling us that the "Honor Cadet" (highest overall ranking at the end of the academy in academics, PT, and firearms) would get to go to the patrol station of his choice (there were no "her's" in my class) after graduation. Everybody else would be assigned to the jail, and, most likely, the jail assignment would be 2-3 years.

Headed To Patrol

So I worked my butt off for 13 weeks. And on graduation day I was named Honor Cadet for Class 127. And I did get transferred straight to patrol…..but it wasn't the patrol station of my choice (at that time LASD had 14 patrol stations). Nor was I the only one in my class to go directly to patrol. Twelve others, for the first time in department history, were sent to patrol as well.

It seems that the Assistant Sheriff's "study" required two-thirds of the graduates of both Classes 126 and 127 to go to patrol so their "performance under stress" could be evaluated. Both of our classes had cadets wash out of the academy, so 13 was the good number. Performance under stress could more easily and quickly be evaluated *at the second busiest policing district in the entire United States*. That would not be *my* choice of patrol station – which would have been Lakewood – but, instead, Firestone. Officially known as Firestone Park Sheriff's Station, Station Number 1, its violent crime rate, on an annual basis, was second only to New York's Harlem.

So it was off to Firestone (FPK) for twelve of my classmates and I, and another thirteen members of Class 126. It would be the best and craziest assignment of my law enforcement career.

CHAPTER IV:

FIRESTONE PARK STATION (FPK):

AN INTRODUCTION

The Los Angeles County Sheriff's Department was founded in 1850. In most places, the Sheriff is the chief law enforcement officer of the county and is charged with maintaining the county jail and serving civil process. In California, Sheriffs provide many more services, including patrol of the unincorporated areas of each county. LASD provided all of its services out of one central location, the Hall of Justice in downtown Los Angeles.

In 1924, the county of Los Angeles, over 4,000 square miles in size, had grown in population, and serving the entire county from one location in a timely manner was no longer possible. The Sheriff created several "substations" in various parts of the county, and each of them had personnel stationed there who could respond quickly when needed. The very first of those substations was the Florence station. In 1955, it was re-named Firestone Park in recognition of the area it served. Firestone Park (FPK) was station Number1. As of

2012, the number of substations is eight times the number created in 1924.

FPK personnel, at the peak of staffing in the 1960's and '70's, numbered over 300. The population served exceeded 250,000 and the patrol area was a patchwork of some forty square miles. It was an extremely high crime rate area, placing either second or third in the nation each year in terms of violent crime per capita. New York's Harlem was always ranked first with either FPK or Chicago's south side second.

In was in Firestone's patrol area that the famous Watts riots began in August of 1965. The catalyst for that deadly and costly riot was a confrontation between a California Highway Patrol (CHP) officer and a black citizen whom he had stopped for a violation. (CHP provides traffic enforcement in unincorporated areas of counties whereas the Sheriff's Department enforces criminal violations such as murder, rape, robbery, theft, etc.)

The year after the riots, and for many years thereafter, the local community "commemorated" the riots with a week-long event known as the "Watts Summer Festival"; more on that later.

In any event, reading the preceding paragraphs should give you some indication of the environment into which twenty-six newly-minted Deputy Sheriffs, including me, were transferred in December of 1968. With so many new personnel being sent to FPK all at once, each of us was told to report to the Watch Sergeant at a specific time on a specific day.

I had never been to FPK before my transfer. My weekend ride-a-long assignments during the academy had included four different patrol stations, but FPK was not one of them. When I drove to the station for my appointment with the Watch Sergeant, I couldn't help but notice the characteristics of the neighborhood around the station. Though the riots had occurred three years earlier, evidence of the violence still existed in the form of burned out buildings and vacant lots where structures once stood before the riots.

Arriving at the station, I parked my cherry 1966 Ford Mustang GT as close to the place as I could. I would later buy a cheaper car to commute to work, as I had visions of my Mustang either being trashed or stolen by those who would quickly determine it was owned by a cop.

A Cheerful Welcome…Not

Entering the station by the back door, I was greeted by several deputies who gave very disapproving looks and who gruffly demanded to know who the hell I was and why I was in their station. They consented to point me in the direction of the Watch Sergeant's office where I introduced myself to the guy with the three stripes on his sleeve.

"Which class were you in, stress or non-stress?" were the first words out of his mouth.

"Non-stress, sir."

His reply got my attention. "Well boy, you ain't gonna cut it here".

I quickly responded, "Sir, I believe I will."

Six years later, he and I wound up working together as Sergeants and became good friends – but during that initial contact at FPK… not so much.

I was assigned a locker, told to get some real equipment (better flashlight, better holster, and combat boots rather than dress shoes) rather than "that shit they gave you at the academy". So my first day off was spent going into debt at Long Beach Uniforms for the equipment I would need at FPK.

Each of us "newbies" was assigned to a training officer (TO). My TO was Deputy Tom Ellis (RIP), and unlike some TO's he actually treated me as a human being. Tom told me he knew I was from the non-stress group and also knew I had a college degree. He said he wouldn't hold either against me if I could prove myself in the field. The opportunity to do so came sooner than either of us could imagine.

Chapter V:

The Early Times

About the second night I worked with Tom, we got a 459 (burglary) in progress call at a local liquor store that had closed for the day. Tom and I took the rear alley while another unit covered the front. Tom told me to cover the southeast corner and he would cover the southwest. Seconds after I took my position behind a utility pole, I saw a subject climb out of one of the liquor store windows and head towards me. He was carrying what looked like a rifle. It was later determined to be a piece of pipe.

When the subject got within ten feet of me, I pointed my county-issued Smith and Wesson Model 15 .38 caliber Combat Masterpiece revolver at him, and yelled in my best "command voice":

"POLICE OFFICER. FREEZE AND DROP IT, OR I'LL SHOOT."

Thankfully the subject did as told, and I yelled to Tom that I had one detained. That was my first ever felony arrest, and Tom was impressed.

One afternoon a few weeks later, I came to work and as soon as I walked in the station it was obvious something wasn't quite right. There were a lot of "suits" there (detectives), and I didn't recognize any of them as being assigned to the station. When I asked one of the veteran officers, he said, "Internal Affairs and Homicide." Seems that a deputy sheriff had just been arrested for an on-duty murder which had occurred not long before my liquor store arrest.

Like my partner and me, the arrested deputy had responded to a possible burglary at a liquor store and encountered a subject inside. The deputy shot and killed that subject. It became obvious that the deceased was a young juvenile, and he was unarmed. To cover himself, the deputy planted a "throw down" gun on the kid and claimed he had only shot after the juvenile had pointed a gun at him.

There is no one more stupid than a stupid cop – in the course of the investigation, homicide detectives were able to prove that the gun allegedly pointed at the deputy had, in fact, been confiscated in a much earlier arrest *by that very same deputy*. The deputy was arrested, fired, prosecuted, convicted, and sent to state prison. Such behavior was not at all typical of FPK personnel.

Good People to Work With

In my years at FPK, I worked with many fine deputies too numerous to mention by name. I will introduce you to three of them: one remains a good friend to this day; the other passed away at way too young an age; and the third was my partner when we reportedly set a record for most felony arrests made in a one month (20 working days) period.

Tim Birkeland and I went to the Academy together and worked together at FPK. It was at FPK that he met his wife Barbara, who was also a deputy sheriff assigned to the station and became one of the first female deputies ever assigned to patrol. Tim and I loved putting serious bad guys in jail so much that we often volunteered to work together beyond the end of our scheduled shift for no pay – just for the opportunity of putting more bad guys in jail….and I must say we were pretty successful.

When Glen Thompson transferred from the Whittier Police Department (where he had been a police officer) to LASD, he was sent to FPK. I was assigned as his training officer, though truth be known, I didn't have to train him much. He knew the basics of police work as well as I did…he just needed to learn LASD procedures and paperwork. It didn't take him long. His family and mine lived in the same general neighborhood, we had kids the same age, and we became close friends. Later in our careers, we worked together as patrol sergeants at both the Norwalk and Carson stations. Glenn left the Department in the mid '70's and opened a business in June Lake, California. He later served as a member of the Board of Supervisors in Mono County, and then as the County's Chief Administrative Officer. He died, way too young, of cancer.

Pat Sullivan was probably the most aggressive (not in a brutal way) cop I ever worked with. In a one-month period, we made 79 felony arrests which, at least at the time, was considered an all-time station record for two deputies working together.

There are a thousand stories I could tell about FPK. In the chapters that follow, I will tell a few.

Chapter VI:
War Stories from Contract Cities

In addition to a large unincorporated area FPK deputies were also assigned to two "contract cities", Cudahy and Carson. A contract city is incorporated and could have its own police department. LASD pioneered a program in which such cities could contract with the Sheriff's Department for law enforcement services less expensively than creating their own departments. LASD had several dozen contract cities, and its program served as a model copied throughout the United States.

CUDAHY

Cudahy was a small, one square mile city that, quite frankly, then and now is an armpit. In the '60's and '70's, it housed two types of people. One type some refer to as "trailer trash" – that is, transplants from down south whose idea of a well-kept front yard consisted of multiple wheel-less vehicles up on blocks. The second type were American Indians (oops...Native Americans) who, unfortunately, fit the stereotype of being combative drunks.

Working Cudahy was not high on any FPK deputy's wish list. For one reason, it was miles removed from the rest of FPK's patrol area, and when backup was needed (which was rather frequently) it was a long time coming. On day shift there was one patrol unit (staffed by one deputy) on duty in Cudahy, and on some days there was also a deputy on a three-wheeled Harley Davidson motorcycle assigned to do parking enforcement. On night shift there was a single two-deputy unit assigned.

As a patrol deputy, I disliked two things. One was being assigned to work traffic enforcement in a contract city, and the other was being assigned to Cudahy for any reason. However, the scheduling sergeant was a fair guy, and he believed that every deputy deserved equal turns in the barrel.

My first Cudahy assignment was as a one-man day shift unit. On my very first day, I received a possible child abuse call at the local emergency hospital. When I contacted the emergency room nurse, she showed me an emaciated 2-year-old whom the mother – a very drunk mother I might add – had brought in because the youngster was bleeding. He was bleeding alright, and the cause looked to be a severe lashing on his butt with a belt.

I interviewed "mom" who angrily and drunkenly told me that, yes, she had hit him a couple of times because he acted up. I told her she was under arrest. She said, "You can't arrest me. I have 6-month-old twins at my apartment, and I have to get back there and take care of them."

At that point, I got Child Protective Services and our juvenile detectives involved, and got another unit to meet me at the apartment. I will spare you all the details because to read them would make you puke. I have never seen such emaciated babies. I have never seen anyone live in the filthy conditions they were in when I found them – and I have seen some very filthy conditions in third world countries, like Haiti.

Those twins were obviously in bad shape, so I asked for an ambulance to respond "Code 3" (that's red lights and siren). They were taken to the same hospital as their two-year-old brother. "Mom" was now under arrest on three counts of felony child abuse/neglect.

Shortly after returning to the hospital with my backup unit, the attending physician told me the twins were in such extremely dehydrated and malnourished condition that he thought they might die. He had already ordered another ambulance to take them to Children's Hospital. Having a six-month-old myself, I was disgusted at what I was dealing with.

About that time, a drunken male walked up to me and announced, "I'm their father. What the f_ _ _ is going on?" I explained to him that his wife (common law) was under arrest, and that the twins might die. His exact words were "I don't give a f_ _ _ if they do, they're a pain in the ass."

 My backup officer saved my job. It was the one and only time in my career that I tried to hit someone because of his mouth. My partner grabbed me by the wrist and said, "He ain't worth your job." And he was right. The satisfaction came from arresting that scumbag along with his wife.

An Unruly Trainee and a Good RTO

About a month before this next incident occurred, I had been assigned a trainee who had just transferred to FPK from the jail. In that month's period of time, I was, to put it mildly, unimpressed with his potential to be a cop. I was particularly concerned because his officer safety skills were not at the level Firestone required in order to survive.

One evening, the Cudahy unit arrested several auto theft suspects; they would be out of service for quite a while, as they had suspects to book into jail and evidence to process. The field sergeant called me on the radio and told me to go to Cudahy while the assigned unit was out of the city. I decided it was a good opportunity to teach my trainee how to conduct a bar check. The High Stakes Bar in Cudahy was the ideal place to teach that lesson – assuming, of course that the trainee followed instructions. (Of course, we all know what comes of "assuming"…)

Before we entered the bar – an establishment known for fights and seriously violent assaults – I coached the trainee on what to do and what *not* to do. For example, I told him, "If you see someone in possession of narcotics or drugs just let me know. We will exit the bar and ask for backup, and when it gets there we'll take action." I carefully explained that just the two of us would get our butts kicked if we tried to make an arrest without a sufficient show of force.

We weren't in the bar 30 seconds when I hear my trainee tell a female, "You're under arrest." He had seen her stash some amphetamine tablets in her purse. We had to fight our way out of the bar, and I was barely able to yell "11-Edward" (our radio call number) into the microphone of our car radio before a great big Indian ripped the microphone cord in two pieces. (This was in the era before we had handheld, portable radios.)

If radio dispatcher (RTO) 36 reads this, I will say again, as I've told her in the past, that she saved our lives. She detected the urgency in the way I said (shouted), "11-Edward", and when she heard no more, she figured we needed help. She knew where we were and she sent ample help our way. That was that trainee's last shift as a patrol deputy.

SHORT FUSE

My last Cudahy war story involves a partner who shall remain nameless. He was a good cop with a short fuse. We were not assigned to Cudahy, but as in the previous incident, the Cudahy unit was tied up and we were sent to handle a "domestic dispute" call. It is a fact, by the way, that domestic dispute calls are among the most dangerous calls that cops respond to. Generally, they involve a male and female and, except for one case I handled in Carson where an itty bitty little Samoan gal punched a male 300+ pound Samoan's ticket, usually the male is the most physically aggressive.

We arrived at the location, actually a well-kept 6-unit apartment building, and knocked on the door of the apartment in question. This was back in the days before our current politicians tried, in spite of our nation's Judeo-Christian foundation, to "normalize" same-sex relationships into "marriage". So when the "person" answering the door looked, from outward appearances, to be male, and complained that "my boyfriend is being a bitch", my partner and I were thrown for just a bit of a loop. Two queers (using the language of that day) fighting was something neither of us had ever dealt with before.

Those readers who, in spite of Biblical teaching to the contrary, feel there is nothing wrong with homosexual relationships, will be pleased to know that we handled this domestic call as we would any other. We separated the parties and determined that no crime had been committed. We admonished them that they needed to get along, and if they couldn't one of them should leave for a cooling off period. We did make it very clear that if we had to come back that evening, one or both of them would likely go to jail. With that, we left.

Now it is important to note that there was an unwritten rule at Firestone: a call was to be handled to conclusion on one visit. Any returns on the same call on the same day were likely to earn the involved deputies a butt-chewing from the sergeant. Our station was entirely too busy with call volume to spend more than one visit on a given incident.

We got about half way back between Cudahy and the north end of Firestone's district when we received a radio call to return to the location we had just left, and "handle to conclusion". That was not a good thing, and to say that my partner and I were both pissed would be an understatement.

When we arrived back at the apartment in question and knocked at the door, the same diminutive "male" answered. (S)he was crying and babbled, "The little bitch cussed at me." That was all my partner could take. He said in a very stern voice, "Listen, you little faggot…." and got not one more word out of his mouth. The little guy threw a punch from out of nowhere and caught my partner square on the jaw, sending him reeling backwards down the steps and smack on his butt on the walkway.

The fight was on and I had my hands full. On the one hand, the little creep needed to go to jail for battery on a peace officer, but for that to happen there had to be a little creep left to arrest. And my partner was doing his best to beat the living daylights out of the guy. Well, all's well that ends well. I got my partner calmed down, and we got the creep in cuffs. No brutality occurred, and when the sergeant noted my partner's bruised chin when we got back to the station, he decided he didn't need to chew us out for not "handling to conclusion" on our first visit.

CARSON

Carson became an incorporated city not long after I went to Firestone, and it chose to contract with LASD for law enforcement services. It was a large and growing city and if anywhere in FPK's area there were any middle class neighborhoods they were in Carson. Eventually Carson grew to the point that it merited its very own Sheriff's station. That was the beginning of the end for FPK, but that is a story for a future chapter.

Carson was sort of an ideal mix of residential, business, and heavy industry. The heavy industry was its tax base and consisted of some very large chemical plants and oil refineries. One afternoon, there was a huge explosion and fire at one of those chemical plants, and when a large storage tank blew up, many people, including a deputy, were burned quite badly. Several plant employees were killed. I responded from the station in a one-man unit (just me folks) when we got the first call, and I arrived on scene just after the storage tank exploded. I found a FPK deputy badly burned who needed to go to the closest hospital ASAP. Harbor General Hospital was just a couple of miles away, so I threw the injured deputy into the back seat of my patrol car and off we went.

Now it was dusk, so I needed to have my vehicle's headlights on. I also needed to use red lights and siren, since I was on an emergency run. And, I needed to advise the dispatcher over the radio as to what was occurring. Well the car I had taken that day was an older one with an old mechanical siren and a dynamotor powered radio. The short story was that every time I keyed the radio mike the engine would die. It was not as quick a trip to Harbor General as I would have liked.

WORKING TRAFFIC

Did I mention earlier that I hated to work traffic enforcement? Well, I hated to work traffic, but so did most deputies. That probably stemmed from our academy class on traffic enforcement where the instructor blatantly stated that the only thing the vehicle code was good for was to provide "probable cause" which, hopefully, would lead to a good felony arrest for an actual crime. LASD deputies worked traffic only in contract cities and, truth be known, did so because traffic fines provided the contract cities with revenue.

Our scheduling sergeant knew that only a few deputies preferred to work traffic cars, and there were more traffic car assignments in Carson than deputies who really wanted to work them. So, being a fair guy, he alternated the rest of us through traffic assignments on a regular basis. My first stint as a traffic cop was unimpressive (at least in the traffic sergeant's mind), as I wrote few tickets but made a lot of felony arrests for dope, burglary, and auto theft arising from the traffic stops I did make.

After that stint in traffic, I was reassigned to a regular patrol unit in Willowbrook which was one of FPK's highest crime rate areas. Just fine with me. After a while though, it was my turn back in the traffic barrel. This time, the traffic sergeant admonished me that if my "stats" (that would be tickets written) didn't improve, my overall evaluation would suffer.

Not being one to settle for a less-than-outstanding performance evaluation, I decided to become a ticket-writing machine. Besides, if I was tied up giving a ticket and a traffic collision happened they would have to give the collision report to another traffic unit…and I hated doing traffic accident reports.

Well, I found a nice little "cherry patch" for writing speeding tickets. It was on 223rd Street, west of Avalon Boulevard. It was a residential area with a school zone, and the maximum speed was 25 mph. However, it was also a very wide, straight road, and was a main thoroughfare across town which avoided the congestion on Carson Boulevard. I would guess the average speed was 40-45 mph so it was ripe for enforcement.

What made my little cherry patch even better was that at the far west end of the three block stretch of westbound 223rd, there was a large curb cut, and on the end of the curb cut facing on-coming traffic was a very large bush. That allowed me to park totally out of sight of approaching motorists with only the antenna of my traffic radar visible. And by the time a speeding approaching motorist could see that radar antenna, it was way too late.

I wrote some humongous tickets there for a week, and the traffic sergeant was "extremely impressed". But when I returned from my days off and went to set up at my cherry patch, I found that someone had cut down the bush which offered concealment for my patrol car. I suspect it was the gentleman who lived in the house I parked in front of, due to the very sly grin on his face that morning.

My very last month on traffic assignment in Carson was not uneventful. I had the "early car" assignment, which meant I had to brief myself at the station rather than attend the shift briefing, since I had to be in Carson by 6 am. One Sunday morning, I arrived in Carson promptly at six and just as promptly headed for Winchell's Donuts for a cup of coffee and some breakfast. Just as I was returning to my patrol car, I heard a very loud explosion, and looking to the west at a nearby housing tract, I saw a big cloud of smoke, flames, and lot of debris blowing into the sky. I responded "Code 3", telling dispatch what I saw. As I entered the housing development, pieces of wood and fragments of cloth and other material were literally raining down on my car. As I turned onto a cul-de-sac which seemed to be the source of the explosion, I saw one house (or what was left of it) completely enveloped in flames; the two houses on either side of it, while somewhat intact, were blown off their foundations. After requesting fire units and ambulances, I got out and approached a man who was sitting in the middle of the street at least 75 feet from the burning house. He was devoid of any clothing, and had obviously suffered critical third degree burns. I asked him what had happened, not sure if he could hear me or respond. But he did both, saying, "I wanted to kill myself so I filled the house with natural gas and lit a match." The insensitive side of me wanted to say, "Well, it looks like you were successful," but I kept my mouth shut. He died moments later. Fortunately, in spite of their houses being destroyed, none of his neighbors was seriously injured.

Later that month, I was on a traffic stop writing a ticket when a woman walked up to me and said something suspicious was going on in an abandoned garage just behind where I had made my traffic stop. She told me that three or four boys had dragged a girl into the garage, and the girl seemed frightened and was screaming. This had allegedly happened just before I made my stop. I hurriedly finished writing the ticket, and told dispatch what I had, asking for a backup unit. As luck would have it, the closest unit was ten minutes away.

If indeed the girl was in trouble, no way could I justify waiting ten minutes to investigate. So approaching the garage I entered through a side door, revolver drawn. Not three or four, but rather *seven* young males were gang-raping a 13-year-old female. I held them at gunpoint until my backup arrived.

LIFE IS FRAGILE

Another Carson experience left a lasting impression on me as to how fragile life is and how precious it is as well. Again I was that 6 am traffic car, and as such was the only unit in Carson when I got the call I am about to describe. LAPD bordered our area, it was shift change for them, and they had no units in their patrol area. The call I received was this: "12T-1 respond to (address in the City of Los Angeles) for a choking baby." I was but 2 blocks away, responded Code 3, and was met at the door by a hysterical father who could only scream, "My baby, my baby!" Entering the small duplex, I saw the mother holding the infant and screaming, "Save her, save her!" I grabbed the child, thinking I'd either have to do CPR or rush her to Harbor General Hospital, just a half mile away. But there was no point. The baby was stone cold and blue, and rigor mortis had set in.

I called my dispatch and asked them to have LAPD expedite their response. Twenty minutes later LAPD showed up to handle the call.

I need to mention that at the time my own wife was very pregnant, expecting our third child. In fact, when I awoke to go to work that morning, I asked her if she thought I should go or stay home, since she was due at any time. She told me to go to work as she didn't think the baby would come that day.

When I cleared the deceased infant call over the radio, my dispatch told me to meet my wife at Kaiser Hospital in Harbor City, but "don't drive Code 3". Well, I didn't, but neither did I waste any time getting there. Within an hour of holding a dead baby, I was holding my newly born and, thank God, very healthy son Brian: a day I will never forget.

COMMENDATION

My final Carson story has nothing to do with traffic. It was the type of call where lots could have gone wrong but, fortunately, nothing did. I was working the 3 pm to 11 pm shift with Glenn Thompson as my partner. On that particular day, we were assigned as 11 E (the E in this case meant we were an "extra" patrol unit). We were assigned a civilian ride-a-long who was a personal friend of Sheriff Peter J. Pitchess and was Vice-President of a very large international corporation. Our "task' was to go anywhere in FPK's area we wanted, respond on any calls we wanted, show this VIP what policing the ghetto was like, and, above all, don't let him get hurt and don't embarrass the department.

Since it was still daylight and the violent crimes in Willowbrook and the North End weren't likely to pick up until after dark, Glenn and I decided to give the ride-a-long a quick tour of the whole station area. As we entered the City of Carson several of the Carson units got involved with a burglary alarm call. So when a "neighborhood dispute – no further details" call was broadcast, we offered to take it, since the area units were tied up.

There are a lot of details I'll skip, but when we arrived the dispute actually involved a portly, elderly, drunken male who was armed with two loaded handguns and was threatening to shoot everyone in sight. We parked in a tactically safe place, told the VIP to stay put, and Glenn put together a "plan" on the fly. We wanted to avoid gunfire if at all possible, as the neighborhood was crawling with people, including dozens of young children, none of whom had the sense to take cover from the man with the guns.

Long story short, I drew the man's attention to me while I took cover behind a parked car. Glenn flanked around behind the guy, rushed him from the side, delivered a crushing blow to both of the suspect's wrists with his baton, and knocked both guns from his hands. We quickly handcuffed him and secured the guns. His wife thanked us profusely for not shooting him as we loaded him in our patrol car for his trip to jail.

Glenn and I made a point of explaining to the VIP ride-a-long that the way we handled the incident *was not* textbook, that we had gotten very lucky, and that we likely would never do it that way again. We told him that under any other circumstances, if a guy with a gun pointed it at us and refused to drop it, he would be shot. We never mentioned what really happened at that scene to anyone at the station, although our report documented it honestly.

About a month later, the station Captain showed up at a briefing and presented us with a Sheriff's Commendation for Valor. The damned VIP must have told Pitchess, is all we could figure.

Chapter VII:

The North End

There was a whole lot more to FPK than Cudahy and Carson. In fact, the best areas to work, from the perspective of a gung-ho street cop were the Florence and Firestone districts (the "North End") and Willowbrook ("The Brook"). Both were high crime-rate areas where responding to murders, shootings, stabbings, rapes, armed robberies, burglaries in progress, and auto thefts was common. And when I say common I'm not kidding. Having multiple murders in one night was not unexpected.

You have to understand the mentality of a street cop: the more activity, the more excitement, the more of an adrenaline rush, the more felony arrests, the better. We lived and breathed that stuff, often volunteering to work overtime without pay at the end of our scheduled shift if "things were hopping" that night. I would add that back then there *was no* paid overtime. There were also no handheld radios worn on the belt, no body armor, and no a lot of things that officers and deputies today take for granted.

The Watts Festival

I worked The Brook, and in the next chapter will tell some true tales of life where the Crips and the Bloods had their beginning. But for now, we'll talk about the North End. The North End was where the riots started, and it is where the annual "Watts Summer Festival" was held in Will Rogers Park at 103rd Street and Central Avenue. Where else but the festival could you find dope dealers stoned out of their minds dealing shopping bags of dope to thousands of people in the park? Making such arrests was as easy as shooting fish in a barrel. Getting your arrestee out of the park and en route to jail without starting another riot was the real challenge.

Where else but "The Festival" could six deputies in a squad, wearing full riot gear, walk right up in broad daylight on a rape in progress occurring on second base on the park's baseball diamond?

Yes, the festival was always a riot in waiting, and in 1969 a mini-riot indeed broke out as someone in the mob of thousands inside the park started shooting a gun. A number of deputies were pinned down behind parked cars on Central Avenue, and a sergeant who was the only one with a "portable" radio (it was the size of a large lunch box) was screaming for help. We shot out street lights with our handguns to keep from being silhouetted by the light.

Now, the folks at the top levels of the LASD and LAPD organizations did not always get along. There was some ego and jealousy involved. But at the street level, cops take care of cops, and LAPD and LASD regularly backed each other up. When LAPD learned we were under fire, they came to our aid. You see, they had planned as if they knew a mini-riot was going to start. They had well over a hundred white-helmeted, baton-wielding cops holed up in a church across from the park. When we asked for help, the front doors of that church literally came off the hinges, an LAPD sergeant with more hash marks on his sleeve than I'd ever seen before yelled "charge", and a wave of blue uniforms stormed into the park with us tan-and-greens right behind them. The park cleared out in a matter of seconds.

The "Festival" was a once a year event. Hot calls occurred daily. Having cops respond to violent, dangerous calls on a daily basis requires good leadership. In my view our station commander, Captain M. Dean Wert, was outstanding. The vast majority of Lieutenants and Sergeants I worked for were excellent as well. They were there when needed but did not micro manage. They enforced the law, policies and procedures and rules. Thus, given the volume of activity, we had few citizens' complaints and few complaints of brutality or racial prejudice, and the good people in the community supported us. The crooks…not so much.

THE SPIRIT OF THE LAW

There is a difference between the "letter of the law" and "the spirit of the law". The letter of the law is what the law says. The spirit of the law is what it is intended to accomplish. Suppose, for example, you stop someone who is speeding "a little bit" and they acknowledge their mistake and are remorseful. If you, as an officer, think you've made your point, it is perfectly okay not to issue a citation. Let me tell you about an instance in which my partner and I may have stretched the spirit of the law just a bit.

We responded to a stabbing and found the victim to be an otherwise healthy male, but with a deep stab wound which, from the sucking sound, had obviously penetrated a lung. Without medical treatment, according to the ambulance crew, he was going to die. Problem was, he refused medical aid and refused to be transported to a hospital. The ambulance crew, and even my partner and I, practically begged the guy to go, but he continued to refuse. His condition was not improving. My partner and I conferred and rationalized that no sober person, when told he would die without medical treatment, would refuse such treatment. Here comes the logic! He was refusing, therefore he must not be sober, therefore he must be drunk, and therefore he should be arrested.

Now, it is important to understand a couple of things. At that time in California, medical treatment could be provided to a person in custody even if they objected. Second, the county would be responsible for paying for said medical treatment which, in this case, would not be inexpensive. We arrested him for public drunkenness and told him he had no choice but to go to the hospital. He complied.

At the hospital, he was rushed into surgery and, long story short, his life was saved. As soon as the surgery was completed, we were notified; then we issued a certificate of release under section 849 (b) 1 of the California Penal Code – meaning he would not be prosecuted. There was, however, the not-so-small matter of a huge medical bill. When the county received that bill, my partner and I would be in deep doodoo if the facts of the incident and our "thin" cause to arrest him were ever known. Now I've always believed in God, but in this case there certainly was a God. Upon his release from the hospital this guy, without prompting, wrote a letter to the Sheriff thanking us for saving his life. He wrote, in part, "I must have been drunk, and they arrested me and took me to the hospital." We never heard a word about the bill.

WOMEN ON PATROL

Our station captain was a ballsy guy. Several years before the Sheriff announced his pioneer "women in patrol" program, we were already doing that (under the radar) at Firestone. Captain Wert allowed several of the interested "lady deputies" to ride as a third deputy in a patrol car. Normally, lady deputies served only as jail matrons or worked the front desk dealing with the public from behind the counter.

We had several outstanding female deputies who were more than anxious to go on patrol, even if they had to do it wearing a skirt and

high heels, and with their handgun and handcuffs in their purse.

One evening, my partner and I had one of our best lady deputies with us in the field. We had found an actual gun belt/holster, etc., that would fit her, and instead of her high heel shoes, she wore some tennis shoes. Looked a little odd, but it allowed her to actually do something besides look pretty. We got a fight in progress call at a local establishment known as the "Chicken Gardens" up on Central Avenue. Three units responded, including ours, and there was a hell of a fight going on. Suspects were swinging pool cues at each other, breaking tables and chairs, and essentially destroying the place. Into the fray we ventured, and as soon as we got inside, a great big drunk charged the female deputy. She waited until the very last second, stepped to the side, stuck out her foot, and tripped the sucker – right through a plate glass window and out onto the sidewalk. Without missing a beat, she was through the hole in the window and had him handcuffed before we knew it.

Now some male deputies were firmly against "letting" females go on patrol. Most of us at Firestone, though, knew that the right females, like the one I just described, could do the job very well.

SETTING A RECORD

The month my partner and I set what some believed to be the all-time FPK felony arrest record (79 felony arrests in 20 working days) was an incredible month. Pat and I had both just finished training new deputies, and as a reward were given three months to work without the burden of a trainee. Even better, we were assigned to work together in the North End, taking a shift that went from 7 p.m. until 3 a.m. It just didn't get any better than that: the absolute busiest shift and with a partner you had total confidence in.

Here's one example of the kind of month we had:

> Start of the shift, we get a call to respond from the station to a possible residential burglary in progress. It's our call to handle with two other units to assist. We get there first and catch four burglars. With help from the other units, we transport them to the station for booking into jail. The whole station area is one hot call after another that night so we are trying to book quick and get back in the field. We no sooner clear the station than we get a possible armed robbery in progress right across the street at a bail bondsman's office. As we pull up, two guys are coming out the front door wearing masks and carrying revolvers. The racking of our Ithica Model 37 12 gauge shotguns convinces them they are about to die. They throw down their guns and throw up their hands. We walk them across the street to the station and book two more felons. An hour later, we stop a stolen vehicle with another four felons. That's 10 felony arrests and we aren't even half way through the shift. Sometimes things just fall in your lap! We round out the night with a felony drug arrest for possession of heroin for sales.

The whole 20 days were sort of like that.

FOOT PURSUITS

My last North End story for this chapter found me working a partner named Dave. Now at Firestone, we had little "gimmicks" we employed to make our job easier. One fairly frequent event was a foot pursuit of a fleeing suspect. You need to understand that in a foot pursuit the bad guy always has the advantage. He can choose where he wants to run, and he isn't wearing a tight fitting uniform with 20 pounds of equipment around his waist (more today, with all the stuff cops carry).

Cops do not like to lose foot pursuits. It sends a bad message to crooks. So at FPK we had a system many of us employed to keep foot pursuits brief. We all carried big M80 firecrackers and a cigarette lighter wedged behind the ammo pouches on our gun belts. If we got in a foot pursuit one of the deputies (whoever was lagging behind his partner) would at some point stop, light the M 80 and yell to the crook(s) "stop or I'll shoot. They seldom stopped….until the M 80 went "BOOM" and then they usually did. Funny how they followed instructions to prone out and be handcuffed!

Occasionally some street punk felon would demand to talk to the watch sergeant upon arrival at the station for booking. He'd claim we shot at him, and the Sergeant would check our weapons. No expended ammo, no smell of burned gunpowder, no gunpowder residue on our hands: complaint unfounded.

Well, one night we were driving down a side street off Compton Avenue and came across a car up on blocks with the wheels being removed. It was a stolen vehicle in the process of being stripped. An upstanding citizen came out to talk to us, and we asked him to call the station if he saw anyone around the car. A couple of hours later we were told by radio that the citizen had called and suspects were stripping the car *now*.

We pulled down the street with our lights out and got practically on top of them before the little punks saw us. But when they did they took off running. I got out of the driver's door and went in foot pursuit. I assumed (bad word) my partner was right behind me. I chased the suspects east bound to the railroad tracks at Graham Avenue, and southbound for a block, and then back westbound on a parallel street. I was in pretty good shape, but I was getting tired and a little pissed at my partner for not doing the M80 trick. Then, all of a sudden, without any "stop or I'll shoot" being shouted, there was a huge BOOM behind me. The suspects hit the dirt, and I covered them at gunpoint until my partner arrived. It took him longer than I expected.

When Dave got to my location, he was cussing up a storm, he was bleeding from the nose, and his uniform shirt was a mess.

"Dave, what the hell happened to you?" I asked.

Seems that when he got out of the radio car, he ran into a telephone pole he hadn't seen, and it knocked him silly…so silly that he got up and ran into it again! I congratulated him on having the presence of mind to cap off the M80. He said, "I didn't, you did."

After we hooked the suspects up and walked them back to our car, we each produced our unfired M80 as proof that neither of us had lit ours off. So what was the "BOOM"?

After booking the suspects, we went back in service and drove slowly down the street where the foot pursuit had ended. As we passed one house, there was an elderly black gentleman sitting on his front porch in a rocking chair. He waved at us and we waved back. We went to the end of the block, turned around, and headed back the way we came. As we approached the house where we had seen the old man, he slowly walked down his sidewalk towards the street. We pulled up next to him and rolled down the window.

He had to have been 85 or 90 years old. In a very low and deliberate voice he asked, if we were "the officers that arrested those young punks a little while ago." We acknowledged that we were.

"Did I help you boys out?" he asked.

We asked him what he meant.

His reply: "Well, I saw you chasing them boys, and I knew you weren't gonna catch 'em. So I fired off my shotgun to see if that would make 'em stop."

We accompanied the old man to his front porch where, indeed, he had a recently-fired 12-gauge that was probably as old as he was. We thanked him for his support and strongly encouraged him to never do that again.

THE CHASE IS ON

Those who watch a lot of cop shows and movies likely get the impression that high-speed vehicle pursuits are a common activity, and might even be thrilling to be involved in. I've been in my share, some of them very hairy, and the truth be known, they are fun to talk about *when they are safely over*. There are some pursuits, such as those occurring in the wee hours of the morning on an uncrowded highway, which pose a threat only to the suspect and the pursuing officer(s). Other pursuits pose a serious risk to innocent people who might be struck by a high-speed fleeing vehicle. I can tell you that in every pursuit of that sort, such a possibility was on my mind, and I prayed, during those pursuits, that no innocents would be hurt.

Fortunately, not many of the pursuits at Firestone turned tragic…not even this one. A Cudahy unit went in pursuit of a stolen vehicle westbound on Florence Avenue and headed towards the North End. That, of course, got the attention of the North End units who readied themselves to assist. When the vehicle got to Alameda Boulevard, it turned southbound, and when it got to Firestone Boulevard it headed west again. At that point things change: the passenger in the stolen vehicle leaned out the window with a gun and fired at the pursuing deputy. A plan was quickly hatched to terminate the pursuit when it got to the railroad overpass at Graham. The means of termination would be shotgun fire, since there was a good backdrop that would prevent stray shotgun rounds from striking any residence.

As the suspect vehicle crossed under the railroad bridge at a high rate of speed, two deputies fired several rounds each at the suspect vehicle. Unfortunately, they missed, but did strike the first two sheriff's units behind the suspect vehicle. No deputies were hit. The pursuit ended when the suspect vehicle took the dips at Firestone and Central Avenue, went airborne, and struck a fence. LAPD got stuck with the crash report since the fence was on the city side of Central.

Another "pursuit" was very slow speed and had a positive outcome, except for my uniform. I was working with a trainee who had been assigned to me for several months. In fact, he was about to get "kicked loose" from training status. Usually the training officer drove and the trainee did all the paperwork, but he was so close to finishing his training, I decided one night to be a nice guy and let him drive while I served as "book man" – the one who wrote reports.

It had not been a real busy evening arrest-wise, but we had taken a lot of crime reports and I still had a few to write with only a half hour left on the shift. Heavy fog had rolled in, limiting visibility quite a bit. I told the trainee to swing by Boy's Burgers so we could get something to drink, and then we'd go park somewhere and I'd finish up my reports. Since it was a cold (by Southern California standards) and foggy evening, I ordered a large hot chocolate.

The trainee pulled onto a side street and turned off the vehicle lights and I began to write reports by the light of my flashlight. I had placed the steaming hot chocolate on the dashboard in front of me. I did tell my partner not to drive off unless he told me he was going to move the car.

I had at least 10 pages of reports and my activity log (we did everything by hand back then) spread out on my lap when all of a sudden, without warning, my partner put the transmission into drive and floored it. The hot chocolate crashed onto my lap, drenching both my reports and a part of my anatomy that was just a bit sensitive. Simultaneously, he was yelling, "They just stole that car! I saw them do it!"

The chase didn't last long as the dummy suspects pulled onto a dead end street. The re-writing of the reports, reconstruction of the log, and chewing out of my partner took a lot longer!

ROUND AND ROUND HE GOES

The final pursuit I'll mention was one that actually had me laughing during the pursuit. Firestone had a couple of old Harley Davidson three-wheel motorcycles (11-Mary-1 and 11-Mary-2) that deputies were assigned to for parking enforcement in business districts with parking time limits. They'd drive along and use a chalk stick to mark tires on parked cars; they'd come back after a designated time had elapsed, and if a vehicle hadn't been moved (and you could tell from the chalk mark), the deputy would write a parking ticket. Those motorcycles were equipped with a two-way radio, but they did not have red lights or siren, just amber warning lights to be activated when they stopped to write a ticket.

One day, 11-Mary-1 came on the radio and said he was in pursuit. I was a block away and I responded. He was in a little housing development that had a circular street…that is, if you stayed on that street and didn't turn off onto the road that led in and out of the development, you could actually drive in circles. That is exactly what I found to be happening. The vehicle being chased was an old pile of junk that I doubt could go faster than 25 mph. Thick black smoke was spewing out of the exhaust, and the engine was making a terrible backfire noise. Behind it was 11-Mary-1 with its amber lights flashing. The deputy was yelling "Stop! I said stop!" between coughing fits prompted by the ingestion of exhaust smoke. It was actually comical.

I stopped the pursuit by blocking the road with my patrol car, but couldn't stop laughing as the motorcycle deputy arrested the vehicle's driver for reckless driving.

JUNK YARD DOG

Let me caution you that if your stomach is at all squeamish you may want to pass on this story. My partner and I were working car 11-Boy on a Sunday day shift. We received a call of an explosion and fire at an auto wrecking yard just south of Firestone Boulevard, and were advised that the fire department was en route. As usual, and this is not a criticism, we beat the fire department there.

We pulled up in front and noticed that the junk yard was surrounded by a very high chain link fence with a sliding gate. The gate was open. We really couldn't see any fire, but could see some light smoke in the area of what looked like a big metal cylinder towards the back of the yard. We made our way towards it on foot.

Now every junk yard in Firestone has one or more junk yard dogs. They are there for "protection". This junk yard was no exception. Between the front gate and that smoking cylinder we saw no less than four dogs, all of which appeared to be a Doberman mix of some sort. What was strange is that each one had what looked like a piece of bone with meat on it, and they were all happily munching away.

When we got near the smoking cylinder, what we saw wasn't exactly pleasant. There was a dismembered body of a male human being which was obviously the source of what the dogs were eating.

The Fire Department's reconstruction of what happened suggested that the victim was using a cutting torch to cut off the end of a large old fuel tank. What he didn't realize was that there was still some fuel and a lot of fumes inside the tank. When the flame from the torch penetrated through the metal, there was a huge explosion and ball of fire. The tank ruptured, and the end peeled back in multiple places. It was multiple jagged pieces of metal which cut the victim into multiple pieces.

In the course of my time at Firestone, I saw people die in a number of ways. This one was unique

BLACK-AND-WHITE TAXI SERVICE

Working car 11-Edward in the North End one night, we happened to be driving east on Firestone Boulevard approaching Alameda Street when we saw a black-and-white police unit pulling out of a driveway next to a closed business. It accelerated east bound quickly, but we could tell it was not a sheriff's unit. Our headlights cast just enough light inside the vehicle to let us see that the officers in that car were wearing tan and green uniforms, just like ours. That would narrow it down to being a South Gate Police Department unit.

As we pulled up next to the driveway from which the police unit had exited, we saw a male subject leaning against a block wall. As we got out to investigate, it was obvious the guy was extremely intoxicated. He told us that two officers had picked him up and then given him a ride, dropping him off where we found him.

Not that LASD personnel would ever do such a thing, but our conclusion was that South Gate PD probably got a drunk-in-public call, and rather than arrest, transport to jail, book the suspect and have to write a report, they served as a black-and-white taxi, got him out of their jurisdiction into ours, and then dumped him for us to deal with.

We asked the subject for identification, and he actually had some. We ran a wants/warrant check on him, and thirty minutes later we were advised he had a felony warrant for armed robbery out of Long

Beach PD. He was not carrying a weapon at the time we placed him under arrest. In talking with him on the way to the station, he told us that the cops who had transported him into our area did not ask him for ID and did not search him before putting him in their vehicle. They missed a good arrest, and given their poor officer safety tactics, could have missed the rest of their lives.

EASIEST HOMICIDE ARREST EVER

We had just cleared briefing for our 11pm. to 7am shift and were headed south on Central Avenue towards our beat in Willowbrook. We stopped at the red traffic control signal at 103rd Street and Central. I was the book man (passenger). Suddenly, from the parking lot of a closed business to our right, we heard the unmistakable sound of gunfire. While bailing out of the car and drawing my revolver, I quickly turned on the spotlight and spun it in the direction of the gunfire. My partner went to the driver's side trunk area of our vehicle, and both of us trained our weapons on the lot. The spotlight shone on a suspect holding a large blue steel semi-automatic handgun. He was standing over another subject who was on the ground. Both my partner and I yelled to the suspect to "Drop the &*%$# gun NOW!" And, he did. We took the suspect into custody; checking the victim, we found him to be deceased.

Why was it easy? Because the crime occurred on LAPD's side of Central Avenue. It was very gratifying to pick up the radio mike to advise dispatch that we had one homicide suspect in custody, and to request LAPD to take the report and conduct the homicide investigation. All it took from us was a little time and a short report on what we saw and did.

TRYING TO KISS OFF A HOMICIDE?

My partner and I were working graveyard shift in the North End. Because we liked to keep up with what LAPD was doing right across Central Avenue, and being the radio guy that I was, I modified a small transistor radio so we could listen to LAPD radio traffic. At that time they broadcast calls city-wide on a frequency just above the AM broadcast band, so the modification was easy.

One night, we heard LAPD 77th Street Station units dispatched on a "man down" call on the west side of Central, just south of Firestone Boulevard. A short time later, we heard their unit arrive and a few minutes later it cleared "UTL" (unable to locate).

About a half hour later, one of our units got a possible shooting victim call on the east side of Central Avenue, just south of Firestone Boulevard. It wasn't our call, but we, along with just about everybody else in the North End, rolled as backup. Sure enough, the handling unit found a deceased suspect who had been shot in the head. They didn't need our assistance, so we cleared.

The field sergeant and one other unit stayed at the scene. About five minutes later, our sergeant requested an LAPD supervisor to meet him at the scene. From the trail of blood and drag marks, it was clear that the crime happened on LAPD's side of the street, and the victim was drug across Central Avenue and dumped in our area. It was merely conjecture, but the suspicion was that LAPD, responding to the man down call, didn't really want to handle a homicide so they "relocated" the victim's body. No way to prove it, but that would be a huge kiss off if it happened.

It Pays to be a Ham

As I mentioned elsewhere, I have been an amateur radio (ham) operator licensed by the Federal Communications Commission (FCC) since I was 12 years old. In fact, it was that hobby that led to my involvement in the LASD Disaster Communications Service, and that ultimately led to my becoming a deputy sheriff. Ham radio operators in most states, and that includes California, can have the FCC- issued call sign as the license plate number on their vehicle. Back then, when knowledge of the International Morse Code was a requirement for licensing it was common for a ham operator seeing another ham operator driving by (as evidenced by the call sign license plate) to tap out "Hi" in Morse code on the vehicle horn. That usually resulted in a "Hi" being sent back.

One day I was working 11-David in the North End. My partner had called in sick, so I was actually working what should have been a two-man car all by myself. At the intersection of 56th Street and Central Avenue, I saw a car with ham radio plates driving slowly ahead of me. Not too many ham operators lived in Watts, but that didn't deter me from tapping "Hi" on my horn as I passed the vehicle on the driver's side. Instead of getting a "Hi" in return I got a questioning look from the driver. It didn't help that the driver didn't look like he "fit" the vehicle, so I slowed down and got behind him. I checked the "hot sheet" which was actually compiled each day by LAPD and listed stolen vehicle license plates. The plate wasn't on the hot sheet, but that didn't necessarily mean much. The hot sheet was often out of date before it was printed and distributed. In fact, I can only remember one time I made a grant theft auto (GTA) arrest based upon a hot sheet entry.

Even though the plate wasn't listed, I was convinced the driver didn't fit the vehicle, so I ran the plate through dispatch to see if it had been reported stolen after the day's hot sheet was printed. It did not come back stolen. As I followed the vehicle southbound, it came to the red traffic control signal at Florence Avenue. I noted that when he slowed to a stop, only one brake light was working. That was all the legal cause I needed to stop the vehicle.

I approached the driver, got his driver's license, and he claimed he had left the vehicle registration at home. While many people don't have their vehicle license plate number memorized, a ham operator with ham plates on his car would know his license number. He didn't. At that point, I was pretty sure the vehicle was stolen.

I had the radio room attempt to contact the registered owner (RO), who, according to the Department of Motor Vehicles, lived in the San Fernando Valley. The Valley was nowhere near Florence and Central. The radio room's call to the RO actually woke him up. When dispatch asked him if his car was stolen he said that it wasn't, that it was parked in his driveway. Dispatch asked him to look to be sure. Moments later he told dispatch it wasn't there and was stolen.

LAPD was contacted to go to the RO's house and take a stolen vehicle report while I "recovered" the vehicle and took the suspect to jail for GTA. That wasn't the only time a stolen vehicle was recovered even before it was reported stolen.

An Unpleasant Task

Upon arrival at the station for day shift, I learned that on the graveyard shift that morning, Deputies Lou Wallace and Al Campbell had been involved in a shooting in Willowbrook. Lou was killed, but not before he was able to fatally wound the suspect. Al was shot and seriously wounded, but was expected to recover.

Any deputy, particularly working a high crime rate area, knew that the potential for line-of-duty deaths was real and always lurking in the shadows. But this was the first time many of us at the station had known and worked with one who was no longer with us. Lou's funeral, a huge tribute, was the first of over 20 law enforcement officer funerals I would attend in my career. I knew more than one of those heroes.

That day, I was scheduled to work a one-man car, unit 17, in the unincorporated south end west of the Carson City limits. However, when last minute scheduling changes required that a unit be "scratched" from the schedule, it was usually one like mine: units in unincorporated areas had less priority than contract city cars. And, if at all possible, maintaining full staffing in the North End and Willowbrook was preferential to staffing cars assigned to little chunks of unincorporated area like the one I was scheduled for that day.

There were a number of things that the station captain needed that day, and I was diverted from my beat assignment in order to serve as "gofer". Lou's personnel file needed to be taken to Administrative Headquarters in the Hall of Justice (HOJ). And while I was at HOJ, I was directed to go to the radio room and pick up a tape of the radio traffic related to the vehicle stop which had resulted in the shooting of Lou and Al.

I headed for the HOJ and first went to the radio room where I contacted the sergeant. He was still making the tape, so I had an opportunity to listen to it. It was chilling, especially the portion where Al was yelling for backup and an ambulance. After obtaining the tape, I headed for Admin to drop off the personnel file.

When I got there, the Division Secretary told me I needed to call the captain at Firestone. Doing so, I actually wound up talking to the station admin lieutenant who told me that before leaving HOJ I needed to go to the Coroner's Office and identify Lou's body. They needed someone who knew him to be able to say that it was indeed him. At that time, the Coroner's Office and County Morgue were in the HOJ. When I arrived there, I identified myself and stated my purpose. A very solemn deputy coroner led me to a viewing area. A dark purple curtain was pulled back, and I viewed Lou's body on a metal table. I made the identification, signed a form attesting to the identification, and left the Hall to return to Firestone.

That was my first experience at having to do something like that. I hoped it would be my last. On the drive back to the station, I tried to put what I had just done out of my mind. It was not safe to be in uniform, driving a marked patrol car through Watts, and be distracted. But, distracted I was, and I would remain so for a few hours.

Chapter VIII:

A Huge Mistake

I'd been at Firestone about a year and a half and knew that it was a good cop's paradise. But I had three young children and a wife at home, and I was not spending a lot of time with them. A friend mentioned to me that the Department's Research and Development Bureau, Administrative Division, was looking for deputies with college degrees who could write. I had my degree, and thanks to my mother – a former newspaper woman – I'd had no choice but to become a decent writer. I actually had a pretty good reputation at FPK and with many detectives because I was a good report writer.

I gave it some thought and actually believed that I could do some good things for patrol if I worked at R&D. I had some ideas for streamlining report forms, etc., and I thought R&D would be a good place to put those ideas into the system. I actually went so far as to go to R&D and meet with the lieutenant to find out more about the job. I'd like to say he's the only lieutenant who ever lied to me, but that wouldn't be true. He assured me that, yes, I could have a real positive impact on patrol operations and procedures if I used my skills at R&D.

I went to Captain Wert and asked his advice. He told me that as a good street cop, I'd go nuts at R&D, that I would wind up doing projects for the brass that had no connection to the real world of police work, and that I would come to regret my decision to transfer. But he told me if that is what I really wanted he'd support my transfer request and give me a good recommendation. I should have listened to him…but I didn't. I put in the transfer request, and just two weeks later was no longer a Firestone deputy.

OJ Simpson

On my first day at R&D, I knew I had been lied to and had made a huge mistake. During the tour of that facility, the lieutenant took me to a large file cabinet, opened it, and proudly pointed to a series of files labeled "OJ Simpson"….that's right: OJ Simpson of USC fame, OJ Simpson of the NFL, OJ Simpson who many believe got away with murder (though that came years later, of course). I guess the look on my face asked the questions, "What are those files and why are they here?"

The lieutenant proudly explained that those were OJ's term papers from USC. They were written for him by R&D deputies. The "quid pro quo" was that a certain Assistant Sheriff received his doctorate degree from USC in exchange for that. I was shocked, disillusioned, and highly pissed off all at the same time. On a positive note, that particular Assistant Sheriff (the same one who got college credits for our stress vs. non-stress academy experience) lost his job a few years later for "misappropriation of county property". No one could have been more pleased than I was. But I digress.

So, before the end of day one, having figured out that I had made a huge mistake, the task was how to make the best of a bad situation and get my butt back to FPK ASAP. For advice I went to Captain

Wert. He could easily have said "I told you so", but he didn't. For a lot of reasons Captain Wert's management style was one I later tried to emulate when I became a chief of police. That style served me well.

Captain Wert looked at me, and I can only describe his look as serious, concerned, and even a bit fatherly.

"Boyd," he said, " you are in a situation far more serious than you realize."

He told me that if I put in a transfer request to go back to Firestone without waiting a few months, I'd be considered "disloyal" by the powers that be, and my career would come to a screeching halt. If I told anyone about the OJ papers, the "movers and shakers" in Admin Division (which essentially ran the Department) would find a way to "get me". That could mean invent a way to fire me, or worse. The advice he gave me, which he said he would have to deny giving, was to wait three months, be a "good company man" and pretend to like my job, and then put in for a hardship transfer back to Firestone based upon the time and expense of commuting from my residence to the Hall of Justice. He said if I could do that, he'd hold a spot open for me at Firestone. Any question why I respected the man? I didn't think so.

Remember my saying that one of my motives for the transfer was to have more family time? Well, that didn't work out at all. You see, the folks at R&D were a bunch of ladder climbers. They figured it made everyone look good if they worked long hours. So we did. And instead of my commute to work being ten minutes like it was at FPK, it was 45 minutes to R&D. Then there was the "informal" – but very enforced – expectation that since we at R&D were all one big happy family we would socialize after work at a local watering hole. Usually that was some cop bar in Chinatown. That did me no good at all. Alcoholism runs in my family, and drinking every night was not a good thing. I'd never done that before, and if I had continued to this day, I would be a dead man. Fortunately, one morning many, many years ago I woke up and as if God had spoken to me I knew I had to stop drinking. And, with God's help, I did – cold turkey. And to this day I have absolutely no desire to ever taste alcohol again.

WRITING THE STANDARDS

In early 1970, there was a lot of heat from the liberals in Congress about "all the riots" that had taken place in recent years in places like LA, Chicago, Detroit, and Newark. And the liberals, as they usually do, attempted to blame the heavy-handed police for starting the riots. In response, President Richard Nixon established the Presidential Commission on Law Enforcement and the Administration of Justice. He directed that Commission to create a "National Standards and Goals for Law Enforcement Report" and he gave a short time frame in which to accomplish the task.

Richard M. Nixon was a Californian and was close personal friends with Los Angeles County Sheriff Peter J. Pitchess. I know that for a fact, because a few years later when I was a detective, I was assigned as one of Pitchess's body guards when the sheriff was recuperating from open heart surgery. I took a phone call for the sheriff at his home one afternoon. The caller was President Nixon.

Not only was Pitchess a friend of Nixon, but so too was LAPD Chief Ed Davis. So, unbeknown to many, LAPD and LASD were assigned to write the National Standards and Goals Report. My three months at R&D found me writing chapters of the final report which were accepted without change. Many of the "standards" for cops contained in that voluminous document were written by a mere deputy sheriff – me.

The timing couldn't have been better. I completed that task, got a bunch of smoke blown you know where by my bosses, since my work made them look good, and I put in my "hardship transfer request" back to Firestone. A few weeks later and I was headed back home to the patrol station I should never have left in the first place.

CHAPTER IX:

WILLOWBROOK

If you've heard of the Crips and the Bloods – and who hasn't – Willowbrook was their birthplace and it all happened in the late '60's and early '70's. In my early childhood, my family had moved to Los Angeles from the City of Long Beach where I was born. My mom's doctor and mine were still in Long Beach. My family did not own a car, so to get to Long Beach for doctor appointments, we took a bus to downtown LA. There we boarded the big red PE (Pacific Electric) train car for the trip to Long Beach. Few remember that at one time LA had one of the world's largest electric streetcar and train systems.

HOW IT USED TO BE

The PE car would go down Alameda Boulevard on the railroad right of way all the way to Long Beach, and in doing so went right through the heart of Willowbrook. I remember looking out the train window and seeing black women wearing long dresses with full length aprons and with bandanas on their heads, hanging laundry on the clothes lines in their backyards which bordered the train tracks. My parents made a point of telling me that those black folks, whose homes were very modest but well-kept, had migrated to Los Angeles during the war looking for work, just as my parents had. Many black families in Willowbrook were ex-military, with the husbands having served the nation during World War II.

When I returned to FPK from my potentially career-ending assignment to R&D I was assigned to a Willowbrook unit. My previous Firestone time had been mostly in the North End with some time spent in the two contract cities. While I had worked The Brook on a relief basis, I had never held a steady assignment there.

How It Is: The Crips, The Bloods, and Common-Place Violent Crime

What a different place that Willowbrook was from the one I remembered a kid! The Brook had become a high crime and high violence neighborhood. The story of the Crips and the Bloods is interesting, as the Brook was their birthplace. There are a lot of stories about the Crips and how they were named for their founder who was crippled and walked with a cane. I honestly don't know if that is true. I do know that one summer Friday night, when the Crips were in their infancy and numbered no more than a dozen juveniles, the Brook units found legal cause to arrest 11 or 12 of them. I do remember one of them walked with a limp, but he certainly wasn't crippled. It was my experience that some of them used canes, but they were carried as weapons and not as assistance to the handicapped.

The Crips grew in number and in age. Instead of going to juvenile hall for their misdeeds, they began to populate the adult county jail system and eventually state prison. It is through their "recruitment efforts", particularly in the state prison, that the Crips grew to not only a national but an international gang. Of course, not all who call themselves Crips necessarily get along with all other Crips. There have been so-called Crips vs. so-called Crips gang wars over issues of livelihood, such as control of drug trafficking in a particular area.

Suffice it to say that what began as a dozen or less young punks is now an international criminal enterprise. The Crips' main rivals are another multi-national criminal enterprise known as the Bloods. They weren't always called that. Initially the Crips' rivals called themselves the "Pirus". That is because Piru Street in the Brook was the dividing line between the two – Crips on one side, Pirus on the other. Some years later the Pirus changed their name to Bloods for reasons I do not know, nor do I care.

MEDICAL CALLS

Armed robberies, serious felony assaults, and murders were commonplace in Willowbrook. That relatively small piece of geography kept more than one ambulance company and more than one hospital busy. All major traumas from there went to St. Francis Hospital in the neighboring City of Lynwood. St. Francis was an excellent hospital with an outstanding emergency room. Any injured deputy would be taken there because the treatment was the best. In fact, a few months after I left FPK for good (as a deputy, since I would return for a brief period later as a sergeant), I wound up in a shooting in East Los Angeles and was hit in the arm. Thankfully, I too wound up at St. Francis, which probably saved my career. That hospital had the neurosurgeon and orthopedic surgeons it would take to reconstruct the shattered bones, nerves, and blood vessels in my arm, making it possible for me to eventually return to duty.

We covered the medical calls that came in, not because of our medical training (though I did once deliver a baby in Willowbrook), but, frankly, to provide the paramedics and ambulance crews with some protection. However, sometimes injuries were accidental rather than the result of gang violence. One afternoon, my partner and I were dispatched to a medical call of an industrial injury at a small wood-processing plant off Alameda Street. In this case, because it was an industrial injury, a deputy would have to write a report anyhow and forward it to OSHA (Occupational Safety and Health Administration – they investigate industrial accidents). We actually arrived on scene before either the Fire Department or the ambulance.

A Mexican worker had been feeding sheets of plywood into a planer. He mistakenly double-fed two sheets at the same time. The top sheet kicked back and struck him right at eye level, penetrating his entire forehead to a depth of several inches. It was an injury that no one could survive. The Fire Department had to cut the plywood sheet leaving just a little more than what was imbedded in his head so he could be transported to the hospital. They knew that if they removed the wood completely from his head he would sustain a massive hemorrhage and die on the spot.

As critically injured as the poor guy was (he couldn't see of course), he was able to respond coherently to the questions I asked him in Spanish. He was able to tell me who he was, where he lived, his wife's name, and their telephone number. Incredible! He died shortly after arrival at the hospital. Over a year later I testified at a civil trial, as the victim's family had filed a wrongful death suit against the company. The machine they had assigned to the victim was defective, and that led to the injury. His family was awarded a lot of money.

My Namesake

This story is not unique, as I know of other FPK deputies who helped deliver babies and had the infants named for them in return. But it is unique when it happens to you. As I just mentioned, LASD was dispatched on medical aid calls along with the fire department and private ambulance company. Besides providing protection, if needed, for the medical personnel, another reason we were dispatched was to issue an EAP form. The EAP was a type of voucher that the ambulance companies would accept to insure they would be paid by the county if the person transported had no insurance or was unable to pay.

In this particular case, we were dispatched on a medical call – a pregnant woman about to deliver – at an address in Willowbrook. That is really not the type of call one wants to be sent on, and when it happens one can only pray that the Fire Department medics or the ambulance will arrive first. That was not to be the case in this particular call. We arrived first and were quickly informed by a relative as we entered the dwelling that the lady was in the process of delivering…*right now*. Checking her, we found that the infant's head was protruding from the womb. We asked the on lookers to get us some clean towels. The ones they provided looked and smelled clean, so we did what we remembered we should from our academy first aid course.

Just after the little one was out of the womb, the fire medics arrived and we were more than happy to turn the baby over to them. As my partner and I were about to leave, one of the onlookers, who I actually think was the new infant's grandmother, came over to us and stared at the nametags we wore on our uniforms.

It was LASD practice at the time that every uniformed deputy wore a name tag with first and middle initials and last name. My given name is Gerald William (though I have always gone by Jerry), so my nametag read G W Boyd. My partner's first two initials were E N. So, grandma says, "We gonna name 'im Gwen." In my haste to hand the baby to the firefighter, I didn't look, but with a name like Gwen, I sure hope it was a girl.

Victims and Suspects can be the Same

One night, dispatch broadcast: "15-Adam handle...*all* Willowbrook units assist...attention 10-Sam, 245...shots fired at a bar in the Brook." (10-Sam was a field sergeant; 245 is a felony assault.)

Upon arrival, we found four guys shot in front of the place, and a couple of others standing in the parking lot holding guns. At shotgun point, those two dropped their guns. The bottom line was that eight people in all were involved and they were all both suspects and victims of felony assault. They had gotten into a beef of some sort, all were packing guns, and they began wildly firing at each other. Those hit went to the hospital, and those that weren't went to jail. Not an untypical Brook incident.

Ride-Alongs

Academy trainees were sometimes sent to FPK for their weekend ride assignments in patrol. FPK deputies were not thrilled at having an academy cadet as a partner. We needed experienced partners for backup, not some starry-eyed kid who might never have experienced anything violent in his young life. Often academy cadets were assigned as a third deputy in a two- man car, and they rode in the back seat. On some occasions, though, if we had multiple cadets on the same night, they would split regular partners into two cars and assign a cadet to each. Such a thing happened to me one night.

It was almost the end of the shift – about 10:40 pm – and I was about to head back to the station. All of the other Brook units had either gone to the station or they were tied up booking suspects. The cadet and I were the only deputies in the Brook. I had just finished thanking the Good Lord that the rookie and I had gotten through the shift okay: a couple of arrests, and a dozen calls handled, all without getting hurt. But I spoke too soon.

"15-David handle, two units and 10-Sam rolling from the station to assist, 254 shots fired, 901S Schaffers at [address]." Let me translate. That means 15-David (that's me and the cadet) handles the call; somebody's been shot, and even though Schaffers ambulance has been dispatched, so has a sergeant. That means they think it is actually a murder.

When dispatch gave the address, I knew the location just happened to be about 30 seconds away from where we were. I turned to the cadet and saw he was madly looking through his radio code book to figure out what we had. I yelled at him to put the book away, summarized what we were about to get into, and told him we were less than a block away and to follow me when we got there.

Now I must explain to all the modern day cops who might be reading this that I KNOW this is not the way such calls are handled today. But back then the LASD philosophy was kind of like the Texas Rangers: "one riot, one Ranger". No, we did not always wait for our backup to arrive (in this case that could have been 10 minutes), and we didn't always call for SWAT. In fact, there was no SWAT until a couple of years after this particular incident occurred.

I pulled up, lights out, a couple of doors away from where the shooting was reported to have taken place. As we were about to get out of the car dispatch said "15-David, be advised the suspect is still inside the location standing next to the RP (reporting party) who called."

As I approached the front door, gun drawn, with the cadet somewhere behind me, I could see through the open doors a female standing in the living room; she was holding a very large revolver. Taking cover by the doorframe, I told her to drop the gun, and she actually did it. I told her to step away from the gun and put her hands on top of her head. Again she complied.

The cadet was right on my tail as we entered the residence. Glancing up a stairway to my left, I saw a male sprawled on the stairs, bleeding profusely from the chest area. I told the cadet to check him for signs of life, and I approached the female. I asked the general question of her and the RP: "What happened?" Note: you can do that without giving Miranda rights.

The female who had been holding the gun said, and I quote: "Dat mutha fucka done be cheatin' on me so I killed da mutha fucka."

As I was handcuffing her and advising her of her Constitutional rights, the cadet came up to me, white as a bedsheet, and practically stammered, "I think he's dead." In my mind I was saying, "No shit, Sherlock; this is Willowbrook. What do you expect?"

The backup and the sergeant arrived and homicide detectives were called. My cadet and I took the suspect to FPK and booked her for murder. I then gave the cadet the bad news that even though it was well past the end of our shift, we weren't going anywhere for quite a while, given the reports we needed to write.

I was off the next two days, and when I came back to work on Tuesday, the watch sergeant greeted me with the news that the aforementioned cadet had reported to the Academy on Monday, resigned, and turned in his gear. Better to find out sooner rather than later that the cop job is not for you. The suspect, by the way, pled guilty to voluntary manslaughter some six months later.

I Hate Tear Gas

If you were to ask which felony crime was the most common in Firestone's area, I'd have to say narcotics offenses of various sorts. Other than that, burglaries of both residences and commercial establishments ranked right up there. Actually the two were related. Burglaries were committed to steal things which could then be sold.

The money obtained from selling stolen property was then used to buy dope.

Responses to burglaries were common, and most of the time, resulted in a report being written. Sometimes the call dispatched was for a burglary in progress, but by the time units arrived, most often the crooks would be gone. Still, every once in a while, the suspects were actually still at the location. In those cases, things got interesting.

I remember a residential burglary in progress on day shift in Willowbrook. I even remember who some of the deputies were who responded. However, I don't recall who was actually handling the call. I know it wasn't me, because I was working a one-man car (Unit 17) in Keystone. But I did respond on the call when the handling unit advised he was 10-97 (on scene) and saw movement inside the residence.

When I got there, efforts had already been made to talk the suspect into coming out by making announcements over the radio car PA system. The suspect(s) weren't going for it. At some point, Field Sergeant Don Kennedy arrived, and it was decided that the use of tear gas would be a good idea.

Back then, a lieutenant was required to authorize the use of gas, and in this case the Lieutenant was Bob Edmonds; he brought the tear gas kit to the scene from the station. I can't recall who fired the tear gas gun (probably good that I can't recall), but I do remember that Flite-Rite projectiles were fired from the 37mm gas gun. It was, I'm sure, just part of the "sighting in" process, but the first round missed the window, struck the exterior of the house, and bounced into the front yard. Fortunately, the breeze blew the fumes away from most of us.

Several rounds made it successfully through the window and into the interior of the structure. We waited awhile with the expectation that the gas would force the suspect out of the residence. Didn't happen.

When tear gas was deployed, particularly the hot burning kind, the LA County Fire Department was on scene in case the building caught fire. Well, there was no fire this time, but after thinking about it for a while, the brass made a command decision. Two deputies would don Scott air packs and make entry to capture the bad guy.

I was selected as one of the two to make entry. Neither my partner nor I had ever worn an air pack, so the fire department gave us a quick lesson. A Scott air pack is not just a little gas mask. It is a heavy, bulky oxygen bottle worn on a back pack and connected to the mask with a rubber hose. I got used to them decades later when I served as a volunteer firefighter. Wearing such a thing restricted our ability to see and to move, and it was very likely to get hung up on something as we moved through the confines of that tiny house.

Just before we put the mask on and started towards the house, the fire guys made a point of telling us we had one half-hour of air, and that after twenty-five minutes, a very loud audible alarm would go off to warn us we were getting low. Of course, that very loud alarm would also give our location away, but we never expected the search of that small house to take a half hour.

So, we made entry and started a methodical room-to-room search. I took the lead and used my baton to poke through piles of clothes and trash that the suspect could have hidden under. My partner covered me with his revolver. We had just one more bedroom to search and we began to do so, flipping over a bed to look under it. Nothing. The only place remaining in the whole house that hadn't been searched was the closet in that room.

Just as I opened the closet door, the Air Pack alarm went off – and it was very, very loud. My partner's went off right after that. We tried hot line, I said, "Have 4-Nora-1 respond Code 3 "(lights and siren), and they were so instructed.

About that time the watch sergeant and the "real" dispatcher came out of the sergeant's office and headed directly towards me. The sergeant had just begun to ask why I was sending an undercover unit Code 3 on that call when Deputy Pickering came over the radio yelling, "Shots fired, suspect down and I've been hit!" Not only did 4-Nora-1 respond Code 3, but so did every unit within miles.

Turns out Walt went to the apartment of the woman in question, knocked, and loudly announced his presence. Getting no response, he tried the door and found it unlocked. Entering, he again identified himself and said, "Are you okay?" He repeated the announcement/question several more times as he went further into the apartment. All of a sudden, a female jumped out of hiding and fired one round from a handgun, striking Walt in the chest. Remember, there was no "body armor" back then like every officer should wear today. Though wounded, Walt chased after her as she fled the apartment, and shot and killed her. He then got to his radio and put out his call for help.

Fortunately, none of the deputy's vital organs were hit. He recovered and returned to full duty.

WHAT DOES IT TAKE?

This seems like an appropriate time to candidly address what it took to be a FPK deputy, how we survived, and how we coped so as not to have serious psychological problems as a result of our experiences.

What makes a good Firestone deputy is answered by defining what makes a good cop anywhere. The difference is that given the volume of activity and the level of violent crime, a Firestone deputy needed to be "on his game" much more frequently than officers in most other jurisdictions. My view of what it took to survive, both physically and mentally, and to perform well, comes from my comparative experiences of having worked for a total of five different law enforcement agencies in my career. It also comes from the input of others, including former FPK deputies.

Here is the list: honesty; integrity; a thick skin; flexibility; objectivity; knowledge of the law, policies and procedures; common sense; awareness and alertness; flexibility, good physical condition; on-going training; and healthy activities and outlets outside the work environment. I would add, particularly in the high stress and dangerous environment that Firestone often presented, that prayer and God's intervention helped a lot.

Firestone was not like some sleepy hollow policing environments, where you could let your guard down – ever. Even when inside the station before or after shift, there was always a perceptible threat. Witness the 2am attack on the station when the Black Panthers threw a fragmentation grenade onto the parking lot. Fortunately, no deputies were injured, but significant damage was done to a number of radio cars.

Maintaining a state of preparation and awareness, as well as adequate physical conditioning, was key to physical survival. In my book *The Will to Live: Five Steps to Officer Survival* (now out of print, but published by Charles C. Thomas in 1980), I cited the example of a Firestone deputy who was shot and killed with his own revolver when, at the end of a foot pursuit, the suspect was able to overpower him, seize his revolver, and then execute him.

Psychological survival was also a concern. It is no secret that cops in general have higher rates of divorce, alcoholism, and suicide than the general public. The violence and gore a cop sees, and which an FPK deputy with any experience certainly saw, can send one over the edge. In my opinion, any of us who worked Firestone for any length of time, and emerged "normal" at the end, owe that positive outcome to a number of things. First, we had understanding support off the job from spouse, family, and friends. Second, we didn't hold it all in; we found ways to talk about things that might otherwise eat at us internally. Third, we had "mindless", healthy outlets off the job that gave our minds something healthy and therapeutic to concentrate on. In my case it was three things: my family (especially my sons, whom I coached in sports); my hobby of ham radio; and being an avid long distance runner (not fast, but long) for most of my law enforcement career. Fourth (but not least, though some will disagree), would be a religious faith which included asking the Good Lord for help when things got tough.

Chapter X:

The East Los Angeles Riots

The relevance of where my family and I lived, as well as the relevance of riots that did not take place within the boundaries of Firestone Station, will become clear. The ELA riots directly impacted our decision to move out of Los Angeles County, and the riots were quelled in large measure to the efforts of FPK responders.

As noted earlier, just prior to graduating from college, I married Patty. We rented an apartment in Inglewood as far removed from the "bad area" and as close to Westchester as we could. My wife had grown up in Westchester, and her family lived there. That apartment suited us well for several years, through the birth of our first son, Chris, and through my time at Central Jail and the Academy.

When I was transferred from the Academy to Firestone, the commute would have been longer and it would have taken me through a big chunk of south-central Los Angeles, which was already a less-than-desirable place to live, work, or drive through. I figured that I'd have to fight crooks at work, and I didn't find much to like about the possibility of having to fight my way to and from work. In addition to that consideration, the wave of criminals had begun, by then, to penetrate even further into the heart of Inglewood, and had encroached too close for comfort to the apartment where we lived. There was no one at our apartment during the day, as my wife was working at Loyola University and her mother was watching our son. But if I were working nights or graveyards, she would be at home alone with Chris. Neither of us was excited about that prospect, given the dangers involved.

I had grown up in Boyle Heights near East Los Angeles, and I certainly did not want to move there. But I knew of an "oasis of safety" in that general area. It was a community known as Walnut Park. It was actually in FPK's patrol area and only a short commute to the station. What made it safe at that time was its physical separation from "the North End", along with the fact that, like areas to the north, south, and east, it was still predominantly Anglo middle class.

Taking Care of Each Other

In the few days between academy graduation and working my first shift at FPK, we found a nice, adequate old Spanish-style house to rent. We gave our notice at the apartment and a month later, on my days off, accomplished the move. One of the advantages – other than the rental house being in a neighborhood that was still safe to live in – was that if I were working the North End, I could swing by the house once or twice per shift; and if I was working day shift or even the afternoon shift, I could see the family for a few minutes. My family had grown, since not long after I began my Firestone tour, Kevin was born, and before I finished my Firestone tour our family was complete with Brian's birth. In addition to my being able to stop by the house, FPK deputies took care of each other and their families. A few of us lived in the station area. A couple of others lived in Walnut Park, and some of the black deputies lived in the

North End or the Brook. We knew where deputies lived and would do drive by "patrol checks" on our shifts.

While the Walnut Park rental served us well during my whole stint at FPK, the ELA riots caused concern. They were a few miles from our home, but it got Patty and me to thinking about several things. Was there really a safe place left in Los Angeles County where we could afford to live? And, where could we live that was safe and where we could afford to buy our first home? Where could we raise our sons that would have nice parks, good schools, and athletic leagues where they could compete? The answer to those questions was Orange County, and, in fact, south Orange County.

MOVING SOUTH

We were not the only "cop family" thinking that way. South Orange County, in spite of a horrendous commuting distance to work in LA, became the choice for many LASD and LAPD personnel, as well as members of the California Highway Patrol. Just weeks after my eventual transfer (this time a good one) to Headquarters Detective Division – Metropolitan Bureau) we moved to a brand new home in one of the first housing developments in Laguna Hills. One of my partners and best friends bought a home right across the freeway in Mission Viejo, making off-duty socializing easy. We stayed in Laguna Hills for ten years, though we moved to a larger home at one point. That location entered into my decision to leave LASD a few years later.

We had been in Walnut Park for a while, and I was enjoying the "Firestone experience". In August of 1970, our sons were growing by leaps and bounds, and instead of cribs or baby beds, we needed bunk beds. So I took a few days off (or so I thought), we painted a bedroom, and on a Saturday, my dad and I took his pickup truck to a furniture store in Whittier to pick up some bunk beds Patty had ordered. On the way back, we turned onto the Long Beach freeway and were passed by several LASD units rolling Code 3. A mile or so later, I saw them exit, and off to our left, I could see a large gathering in a park just east of the freeway. I could see people throwing items at helmeted deputies who had already begun to deploy tear gas to disperse the crowd.

When I arrived home just fifteen minutes later, Patty told me the station had called, and I needed to report for duty ASAP. I went to the station immediately, leaving Patty and my dad to unload the furniture. So much for vacation days! In fact, I didn't get home again for nearly a week.

GOING TO EAST LA

As I walked in the back door of the station, before I could even ask what was going on, the watch sergeant saw me and said, "Boyd, you grew up in East LA, didn't you?" My answer, of course, was yes.

"Good. You're in the lieutenant's car. Gear up. Your squad is leaving for East LA in 5 minutes."

As I ran towards the locker room, he yelled, "And make sure you have your helmet, baton, and gloves." Note: no upstanding FPK deputy would ever go in the field *without* those items, and particularly not to a riot, which was what I assumed we were headed to.

A little background on the "event" before I discuss the deployment: A group of Hispanics had a parade in ELA that day to celebrate Mexican Independence Day. Some of those marchers were of the same frame of mind as some of today's radical Mexican groups, like La Raza. They didn't mind being in the USA for jobs, but they really wanted where they lived (and most of ELA was Mexican) to be a "little Mexico". The parade, perhaps better described as a protest march, went from a large park near ELA Sheriff's Station to another park a few miles away. ELA deputies monitored the march and actually assisted with traffic control so that the marchers and their few floats would not have to stop for red traffic lights.

In repayment for LASD's helpfulness, deputies inside the park at the end of the parade began to be assaulted, hit with rocks and bottles, and hit with wood broken from park benches. Those deputies at first requested three units to assist Code 3. It soon became evident that that wasn't going to be enough, as all deputies on site where being pelted with thrown objects, and hit with punches from multiple suspects. In addition, several deputies had to fight for their lives as rioters tried to take away their handguns. "Three units, immediate assistance" progressed to a 997 ("all area cars needed Code 3") and eventually a 999, which is "all units respond".

I must tell you that at FPK our egos, and the way we did business, seldom resulted in a 997 being requested. In fact, I only remember that happening once. And I never heard a FPK-initiated 999, even when a deputy was involved in a shooting. But the 999 in ELA that day was definitely warranted.

THE RIOT SPREADS

The confrontation in the park soon spread to a nearby business district and eventually throughout most of ELA which included large business districts on Whittier Boulevard and Atlantic Avenue, as well as residential neighborhoods. It took a week of effort before the riot was fully quelled.

Back at Firestone, three other deputies, myself, and the lieutenant took off in the lieutenant's patrol unit. I was assigned as navigator since I knew ELA streets well. The lieutenant asked whether I spoke Spanish, since that might come in handy, and I told him I did. Four Firestone units, each with four personnel, made up the lieutenant's squad and we headed for ELA. Before we even got there, the radio room sergeant was giving us what, today, would be called a "mission assignment". I would add that when we left the parking lot of FPK, the lieutenant's new patrol car, a 1970 Plymouth Fury, had a total of 71 miles on the odometer.

By the time we left Firestone, the rock- and bottle-throwing in ELA had turned into a scene of rioters throwing Molotov cocktails, looting businesses, and then burning down the businesses they had stripped clean. LA County firefighters had been sent to put out the dozens of major fires that eventually turned into a conflagration that devoured entire city blocks. The firefighters came under small arms fire from rioters on rooftops shooting at them with rifles.

A New Car...But Not For Long

Our first "mission assignment" was to rescue a company of firefighters who were pinned down by gunfire on Whittier Boulevard about a mile from where the riot had started. As we got to ELA and began driving eastbound on Whittier Boulevard, it took less than one block before bricks thrown from rooftops had smashed out every window in the vehicle and dented just about every piece of sheet metal on it. We'd have asked for backup ourselves, except that we *were* the backup. Our driver did a heck of a job getting us through it, but all of us, including me, were cut and bruised from both broken glass and flying objects which found their way into the vehicle interior.

When we arrived at the assigned location, we could see that the firefighters were still taking fire. They had taken cover behind their engines, but rounds were hitting the trucks with a "ping, ping, ping". As we exited our vehicle on the side away from where the gunfire was originating, we developed a plan. One other deputy and I laid down cover fire towards the rooftop from which the "enemy" was firing. While the shooters stayed down, we got the fire fighters to hop in their engine and get the heck out of the area. Once the fire department had left, we got into our vehicle and did the same.

The first twelve hours we were in ELA, we went from one "officer needs help" call to another. Officers from many outlying police departments like Pasadena, Vernon, Huntington Park, LAPD, etc., had responded, and even with all that help, quelling the riot was no easy task. It was not uncommon for us to take a hit on our vehicle from a Molotov cocktail, and when we got out to chase the suspect, someone else would open up on us with a firearm. One time, a bullet struck the door post as I was getting out of the vehicle. I really thought that was a little too close for comfort.

Sometime around 3am, we were driving by a Catholic church when a group of rioters threw a Molotov under our vehicle. We quickly drove over it to safety, and bailed out of the car to catch the suspects. They ran to the church, and a priest in his clerical attire opened the door to let the suspects in, and then closed it as we approached. The priest yelled, "Viva la Revolución" ("long live the revolution", which was the slogan of the anti-USA rioters) – absolutely unbelievable to me, a life-long Catholic! He then yelled at us that we could not go in the church, as he had granted the rioters "sanctuary". Unfortunately, he was right, but that did not stop me from royally cussing out a priest for the first and only time in my life.

About 4:30am, things died down quickly. I guess even rioters get tired. The commander in charge of the riot response, who I think by then was the Patrol Division Chief, began to assign squads to various places where they could go out of service and get some sleep. We were assigned to a small LA County Fire Station which housed only one engine and a crew of four. Of course, even if the firefighters were willing to give up their beds, four beds do not sleep sixteen deputies. In fact, for most of the five days we were in ELA, a concrete floor served as a bed.

IT PAYS TO HAVE FRIENDS

Before heading to the fire station, it became very clear that we were all very, very hungry. No Winchell's Donuts, McDonalds, 7-11 Markets, or anything like that was available, and we were starving. It suddenly occurred to me that the family of a good high school buddy of mine owned a Mexican restaurant on the edge of the riot area. It was very early in the morning, but it was worth a chance. Sure enough, even though the business was closed, it was occupied – by the owners, who were guarding it with a shotgun to prevent arsonists and looters from destroying what they had spent decades building.

I knocked at the door, and though it had been close to ten years since I had seen Señor Garcia, he recognized me. Not being of the same mindset as the rioters, he first thanked me for what we – la policía – were doing. I explained that we were very tired and hungry, and within ten minutes, he had warmed up some tamales and rice for us. Muchas gracias, amigo!

After catching a few z's at the fire station, we went back in service. Through the grapevine we learned that a sheriff's unit from Lennox Station had been set on fire during the night while the deputies slept at another fire station. Better them than us. If our car had burned, a whole arsenal of weapons and ammo would have gone up, too. Before we had left FPK, the Lieutenant had a deputy clear out the station armory and load everything in the trunk of his unit. Our long guns were old (but valuable), and consisted of some turn of the century .30-30 lever action carbines and several Reising sub machine guns.

YOU ATE WHAT?!

By noon on day two, we were informed that food would be served in a chow line in the park next to ELA Sheriff's Station. The tamales and rice had worn off, and we looked forward to something to eat. Since I was in the company of a lieutenant we moved up in the chow line rather quickly. The food turned out to be box lunches prepared by jail inmates and served by jail inmates.

It was pretty clear, once the boxes were opened, that the inmates knew those lunches were going to cops. They didn't poison us and, yes, the apple and cookie were edible. But they screwed us bad on the sandwiches. Have you ever been offered a peanut butter and ham sandwich with dill pickle and catsup? I dare you to eat it. We didn't.

One lieutenant – and *which* lieutenant was only rumor, so I certainly won't name names even at this late date – took one of the lunches and put it, intact, where he could get to it later. Sometime later, Sheriff Pitchess himself came to ELA Station to visit the troops. He asked if the troops were being fed and, of course, his "yes man" staff assured him that we were being well taken care of. *Au contrare,* said the lieutenant, who then provided the Sheriff with the aforementioned box lunch. Upon opening the box, according to witnesses, Sheriff Pitchess, who was known for uttering a profanity from time to time, flew, into a rage. From that point forward, deputies on riot duty ate hot chow – not only edible, but actually quite tasty – served from a buffet line, and served not by inmates but by Jail Division brass. Loved it!

The riot eventually fizzled out. There wasn't much left to loot or burn, and some of the rioters themselves had been injured and lost their steam. Even when the riot was over, though, controversy continued. In spite of videotape to the contrary, the militants accused the Sheriff's Department of starting the riot, and the whole situation was not helped by the fact that a well-known Mexican journalist was accidently struck and killed by a tear gas projectile fired into a bar from which shots had just been fired at deputies. Poor guy was just sitting at the bar having a drink when he lost his head….literally.

While some were blaming the Sheriff's Department for starting the riot, the business community, including many Mexican-American business owners, were blaming the Department for not doing enough to prevent looting and arson. It was a no-win situation. However, community outrage was put to good use by the Sheriff in preparation for the ELA Riots Part II which would happen a year later.

CHAPTER XI:

THE EAST LA RIOTS PART II

Following the August 1970 ELA riots, the Department's Intelligence Unit started paying a lot more attention to some of the activist groups in ELA. It was clear that they were heavily influenced by the Communist Party of Southern California, were very anti-USA, were quite militant, and were becoming heavily armed. That intelligence paid off when it became clear that they were planning another protest march on the anniversary of the first ELA riot. This time the Department would not be caught by surprise. LASD would be prepared to respond quickly and decisively to any eventuality.

It became clear that this group of subversives was planning to march from several different starting points scattered around southern California. That three-day march would culminate with a parade and rally in ELA on a specific date, time, and location.

TACTICAL PLANNING

LASD, in conjunction with LAPD, tasked some of their best tactical minds with developing a strategic plan to rapidly quell any attempt to start another riot. Some of the LASD lieutenants charged with planning were former combat veterans of the Army and Marine Corps. The plan they developed was superb, and, as you will see, highly effective. It is without a doubt the best-planned and best executed operational response I have ever been honored to participate in.

Based on undercover officer infiltration of the subversive group, as well as paid informants, the LASD Intelligence Unit determined what the march organizers had planned, and that information was quickly conveyed to our tactical planners. The tactical plan for the marches from outlying areas to ELA was simple: We knew the routes of their marches; for the three days of these marches, the groups of protesters where paralleled by a compliment of deputies two platoons strong. The protesters had no idea that they always had nearly a hundred deputies within half a mile of them. The idea was that if they started a riot on their way to the riot, we could respond quickly and knock it down before it went very far.

As I recall, there were four separate marches underway from various parts of the county at the same time, and each march was three days in length. That meant 400 Sheriff's personnel plus logistical support was committed to monitoring the marches. Undercover Intel deputies made regular reports as to the tone, demeanor, and apparent intent of each group of marchers.

Along these routes, deputies would leapfrog from one staging area to the next. The one I was involved in was the march from San Pedro to ELA. We staged at the Long Beach Drive-in (yes, they still had drive-in movie theaters back then) on day one, an aerospace company hanger in Downey on day two, and at the Floral Drive-in on a hill above ELA on day three. At each of these staging areas, we practiced our crowd control and baton tactics. In the early morning hours of the day of the ELA parade/protest, all eight platoons snuck into the Floral Drive-in and were joined by nearly 250 more deputies. That equaled about 150 Sheriff's patrol vehicles with four personnel per vehicle.

On the final morning before the "parade" started, the Sheriff met with ELA businessmen and community leaders. He told them straight up: "When this parade starts you will NOT see any deputies. If the marchers start a riot it won't be because we did anything. If they start a riot, burning and looting as they did last time, you are going to ask me to put a stop to it. Unless you ask, I won't. And if you do ask, you'd better own up to it afterwards."

"Yes, Sheriff," was the response.

THE CHARGE OF THE SHERIFF'S BRIGADE

About two blocks into the march down Whittier Boulevard, things got out of hand. The militants just couldn't keep from looting and burning, and the local community representatives and business owners pleaded with the Sheriff to stop it.

At the Floral Drive-in, the gates opened and 150 black-and-white Sheriff's units with lights and siren took off for Whittier Boulevard. When we hit the Boulevard we drove at the rioters at high speed, screeching to a halt just in front of them. Four deputies per car with batons at port arms charged the rioters. The rioters fled. The first rank of patrol cars had been parked in such a manner as to leave room for the second rank of patrol cars to come through and "leapfrog". Again patrol cars were driven right up to the fleeing rioters and the scene was repeated. Those few idiot rioters who tried to stand their ground or tried to throw something at a deputy got hit and they got hurt. Each injured person takes two more to drag him away. That, combined with fresh deputies every 100 feet running rioters to exhaustion, caused ELA Riot II to be over in less than 45 minutes. And in the 40 years since then, there *has not been another riot* in ELA. The leapfrog tactics used were a stroke of genius. It was a thing of beauty.

The communists who organized the second riot tried to generate heat on the Sheriff's Department. Community leaders and business owners, themselves Hispanic, came to the Department's defense, praising us for keeping ELA from becoming an inferno for a second time.

Chapter XII:

Some Miscellaneous Stuff

As much as I have tried to organize this book into some kind of meaningful order, there are a few stories that either didn't fit elsewhere, or I simply forgot to put them in their right place. One such story has to do with the Black Panthers.

I mentioned elsewhere that in the '60's the Panthers were a very subversive, violent, and dangerous anarchist group. I guess our federal government today doesn't view the "New" Black Panthers the way the government did back then, because our current President and his Attorney General have refused to prosecute the Panthers for well-documented violations of federal voter intimidation law.

Back in the '60's the Panthers were cop killers. As I have already noted, they tried killing deputies at Firestone with a frag grenade. They brutally murdered cops in many cities across the country. In California alone, they ambushed and killed cops in San Francisco as the officers sat in the station writing reports, and they killed an officer in Oakland from ambush. The suspects in the Oakland murder were identified by name, and I bet every cop in California was looking for those guys. I know my partners and I at FPK were.

Since the Oakland Panthers were known to take pride in their dapper appearance, on a hunch we began contacting clothing stores and dry cleaning establishments in our patrol area, showing them photos of the suspects and asking if they had seen them. Now, all of the owners of these establishments were black, and though most of them were law-abiding and supportive of cops, they were scared to death because of the brutality of the Panthers. Many we talked to were obviously afraid of even discussing the subject. One day, however, my partner and I went into a dry cleaning shop just off Central Avenue and showed the pictures; the clerk told us one of the suspects had been in the business an hour before.

We obviously shared that info with our Department and with LAPD, and it seemed like every day for a week, one of our two Departments just missed the suspects by a few minutes. They were eventually caught, but not by us. Had I been so fortunate, it would have ranked as the top arrest of my career. I don't like murderers. I hate cop killers.

Panther Headquarters

The Panthers had a southern California "headquarters" on Stockwell Street in the City of Compton. I shouldn't bad-mouth Compton PD, because for one thing that department no longer exists. Compton is now a contract city of LASD. Back then Compton PD officers, with rare exception, were useless as tits on a bull. They knew the Panthers were in their city, but they couldn't have cared less and did nothing to discourage them. LASD, on the other hand, paid lots of attention to the pig-hating Panthers. Not a shift went by that multiple LASD units did not go by the Stockwell address. We'd park in front just to piss 'em off. If anyone was coming or going from the Panther house, they got contacted, run for warrants, and generally inconvenienced to the extent allowed by law. On more than one occasion, either my partner or I would walk up to the front porch and grab one of the Panther newsletters that were free for the taking.

Eventually, LASD and the FBI served search warrants on the Stockwell location. What they found convinced a number of us that we were dealing with more than we realized. In an upstairs bedroom, they found a military model machine gun that was aimed at precisely where we used to park our patrol cars when we "visited" the Panthers. They also found an extensive network of underground tunnels which went for several blocks away from the Stockwell address. Obviously they had a means of coming and going to escape detection, and an escape route if a gun battle ever broke out.

Paid Overtime

Speaking of Compton, that city had a municipal airport. The airport was constantly suffering burglaries to the office, hangars, and aircraft. Lights, including runway lights, were being shot out. Not only were the consequences of these criminal acts dangerous, but they were very costly – so costly, in fact, that the City of Compton, even though it had its own nearly useless police department, contracted with the Sheriff's Department to provide on-site security at the airport during hours of darkness.

For my entire law enforcement career, I have never worked at a rank where there was paid overtime. About a month after I was promoted to sergeant, deputies finally began to be paid for their overtime. I missed that opportunity. And, of course, in my time as a sergeant, lieutenant, captain, and chief, there was a lot of overtime, but none of it paid.

The exception to the rule was that if we worked the Compton airport security detail on a night off, we would get paid. As I had a growing family, I jumped at that chance whenever I could. Besides, at one time I had really wanted to learn to fly, and had even completed ground school and had a few hours in a Cessna. It was sort of neat to be able to check out the hundred or so aircraft that were based at Compton.

We'd work the assignment in pairs, each of us with our own patrol car. They gave us the high mileage "beaters" for that assignment, but we didn't care. Many a night after the airport closed at midnight and no inbound flights were expected, we'd drag race those patrol cars down the runway just to see what they'd do.

The only real excitement I ever had in all the times I worked the airport was one night when a carload of gang-bangers drove by and started shooting out parking lot lights. I guess they didn't know we were there, but they sure found out quickly. Unfortunately, arresting them didn't help our "stats" for the month, since arrests made at the Compton Airport didn't count.

HIT BY AN AIRPLANE

The incident I am about to relate did not involve me, but I know it happened because I saw the evidence the next day. When two deputies worked the airport they would take a nap, one at a time. If something required the sleeping deputy to awake, he'd get called over the radio, and of course sleeping deputies left the radio volume on high. One night, rather late, a deputy pulled between two hangars to sleep and turned off his vehicle's lights.

The second deputy also fell asleep at the same time, which certainly wasn't part of the plan. Therefore, neither deputy was aware that a single engine private aircraft had landed and was taxiing to its hangar. It turned between the two hangars where sleeping deputy #1 was parked, lights out. Before the pilot could stop his aircraft, the propeller chewed through most of the patrol car's trunk. Rumor has it that the deputy occupying that car required a change of pants immediately thereafter.

A Cop Gone Bad

The following story is tragic in several ways. I tell it because it is one of those incidents that I will never forget. I was working the 3pm to 11pm shift and arrived for briefing at the beginning of the shift. The sergeant giving the briefing looked very solemn and upset as he started the briefing.

"Gentleman," he said, "a couple of hours ago we had a murder in the south end, and it looks as though the suspect is an on-duty sheriff's detective sergeant."

He went on to name the suspect, whom many of us knew, as he used to work Firestone before he transferred to Headquarters Detectives. Though we didn't need it because we knew the suspect, he gave us all a picture. The suspect vehicle was an unmarked LASD detective unit, and he gave us the description and license number.

This particular sergeant, who had been on duty that day, had stopped by his house at lunch time. He found his wife in bed with another man. Using his service revolver, he shot and killed them both. Neighbors had heard the shots, saw the sergeant get in his car and drive away, and called FPK. Responding deputies discovered the victims.

It was believed that the sergeant might still be somewhere in Firestone's area, perhaps a remote area, and might have or be contemplating suicide. In any event, there was an all-points bulletin (APB) out for him, and he was to be considered armed and dangerous. Numerous efforts had been made to reach him by radio on all LA County Sheriff radio channels. He had not acknowledged those efforts. Each of the units of our shift was assigned specific parts of our area to search. My partner and I were assigned to the Dominguez Hills. That area was the most remote part of the station area. If he was still in Firestone, it was likely he would be there.

As we went in service, we were greeted on the radio by repeated APB's for the suspect, and repeated pleas over the radio by one of his closest friends on the Department to give himself up. An hour or so later, we were told to hold all of our non-emergency radio traffic as they had an emergency on Frequency George. Our patrol car that day was one of the newer ones, and, unlike many, had a radio with all of the LASD frequencies in it. We met up with another Firestone unit, and they kept their radio on the Firestone channel so neither of us would miss a call; on our radio we all listened on Frequency George while his friend negotiated the sergeant's surrender over the radio.

As it developed, the Sergeant had driven some distance from Firestone and was parked on the parking lot of the courthouse in Pomona at the far east end of the county. After another hour or so, a broadcast was made that the suspect was in custody.

COVERING FOR EACH OTHER

Speaking of Pomona, that city has had its share of riots though none on the scale of LA or ELA. One summer there was some racial unrest there, a riot started, and Pomona PD needed help. The first radio broadcast we heard was for Sheriff's units from San Dimas and Temple stations to respond. At that point, our field sergeant asked for all north end and Willowbrook units to meet him at Rosecrans Boulevard and the Long Beach Freeway. When we all got there, he told us which units would go with him if FPK was requested to respond to Pomona, and which units would stay back and handle calls. Mine was one of the stay-at-home-and-handle-calls units (DARN!).

A short while later, the radio room sergeant came on the air: "ELA and Firestone designated units respond to the 999 [officer needs help big time] in Pomona." Off they went. But about fifteen minutes later, long before even the fastest FPK units could get to Pomona they cancelled the response, saying, "All Firestone units, return to your area."

Now those of us who remained at home *knew* that FPK units (that sergeant and those deputies in particular) would never miss a riot. So we *knew* that they would not cancel their response. We *knew* they would keep going in the hopes that there would still be some action left when they got there. The problem was that our station dispatcher and the radio room *did not know* what we knew. Therefore, they began to assign calls to units they assumed had returned to Firestone. Without anyone saying a word, those of us who were in Firestone began to acknowledge not only our own calls, but we also used the call signs of the missing units to acknowledge and handle their calls. And without anyone saying anything, the units which eventually did get to Pomona and did get into a little action *knew* that we would cover for them. That's just the way Firestone was. In spite of us trying to change our voices over the radio depending on whether we were acknowledging our call or someone else's, I'm sure the RTO's wondered why Firestone 11 suddenly sounded like Firestone 11-Adam.

Chapter XIII:

Another Look

In early 1971, I decided it really was time to transfer out of Firestone to gain more and different experience in other aspects of police work. Firestone had been good to me. I'd served as a patrol deputy and had worked with some of the finest law enforcement officers one could hope for. I'd been a training officer with all the extra work and frustration that goes with it. I had served as an acting watch sergeant on occasion, had worked the front desk, and for a few months had served as Administrative Aide to the Captain.

Detectives

This time instead of thinking I knew where I should try to transfer – recalling the debacle of my previous move – I asked some lieutenants and the captain for advice. The captain knew that I wanted to promote at some point, and he was right, though I did not have a "plan" for that like some of the more upwardly mobile types. The captain and lieutenants all agreed that detective experience was the next logical step, and the easiest way to get that would be at Headquarters Detective Division – Metropolitan Bureau. Metro had recently taken on some special projects including assisting both the Homicide and Intelligence units with the on-going Charles Manson investigation; and so they were looking for new staff. I applied and was accepted.

Metro was a pool of detectives that would assist any patrol station or any other detective unit when requested. One of my first assignments at Metro brought me back to Firestone. A Firestone deputy, Gary Saunders, had been murdered, and threats had been made to kill a witness to the murder. We were assigned to guard the witness's house 24/7/365. Not glamorous duty, but you know what? It was Firestone. So while sitting in an unmarked car in front of the witness's house, we managed to make felony arrests for one thing or another on a regular basis.

My Job is not Worth $1000

We rotated in and out of that assignment while working other cases. On a case that didn't originate in Firestone, my partner and I were working a burglary surveillance in Marina Del Rey in the Lennox Sheriff's Station area. We stopped a VW "bug" that we had probable cause to believe was being driven by a burglary suspect. In the course of the stop, we encountered a very large amount of cash, a *lot* of drugs, a loaded .45 semi-automatic, and a list of "customers".

We transported the suspect and all of the evidence to Lennox Station. Our sergeant directed my partner and me to book the gun and narcotics into evidence, while he counted the cash and booked it into evidence. Hours later, after all the reports were written, I got in my car and headed home.

When I pulled into my garage, the light came on and for the first time I noticed a plain white envelope on the front passenger seat. I hadn't remembered it being there before, and I opened it. There was $1000 in cash in that envelope. I got a very sick feeling in the pit of my stomach.

I went inside the house and tried to get a hold of my sergeant (but this was before cell phones) and couldn't. I called the Headquarters Detective Division watch commander and explained that I had $1000 that wasn't mine and that I felt somehow it was connected to the arrest we had made in Lennox. He knew I lived near Firestone, so he had me take the money to the FPK watch commander to put in the safe. I was advised to return to FPK in the morning and write a report about the money. He told me that my sergeant would meet me there in the morning.

I went to Firestone as instructed. The Detective watch commander had already called the FPK lieutenant, who I knew well, of course, from having worked there until recently. As he was counting the money prior to putting it in the station safe, he asked me a very pertinent question. If it was intended as a bribe from one of the dope suspect's cohorts, how would he know which car was mine? I hadn't been near my own car since well before we made that arrest. The sick feeling in my stomach got worse. I decided to write my report then, not in the morning. As I was writing it, the lieutenant got a phone call from the Detective Division watch commander, informing him that my partner had also found an envelope with money in his personal vehicle, and he was en route to the station nearest his home to do what I was doing. The Detective watch commander asked to speak to me. He had one question: Who counted the money from the arrest and who put it into evidence? I told him my sergeant had taken that task. He again told me to report to FPK at 8am the next morning, and someone would meet me there.

At 0800 the next day, I pulled into the parking lot at FPK and saw my partner from the day before walking towards the back door. I hastened to join him. Before we could get in the door, we were yelled at from behind. We turned to see our sergeant. He was disheveled and red in the face, and was yelling at us that we were ungrateful %$#&&^ who had f***ed him up. He went for his waist band as if going for the gun under his jacket.

About that time, two FPK deputies who knew me but had no idea who the sergeant was, jumped him and removed his hand from the grip of his revolver. They disarmed him and took him into the station. A short time later, the Detective Division Chief arrived along with several Internal Affairs Investigators. After interviewing the sergeant, they contacted my partner and me.

The sergeant admitted stealing money from the doper's cash. He kept some and put the envelopes in our car "as a reward for doing a good job". He was relieved of duty pending completion of an investigation. Unfortunately, not long afterward, that sergeant committed suicide. If my two former FPK partners hadn't intervened on the parking lot, the sergeant might have committed murder, and my partner and I might have been the victims.

SCARING YOUR PARTNER

The detectives I worked with at Metro were, with a few exceptions, pretty solid street cops, though some of them came from patrol stations with much, much less activity than Firestone. Over the next few months following the dope incident, I worked cases all over the county and with different partners. Usually if there was a case we needed to work – let's say in Newhall – we'd go with a Metro detective who had worked that station and knew the area. Likewise, when a case came up in Firestone, I or one of the other guys with Firestone experience would go along with someone who hadn't worked FPK.

I was assigned to one case in Firestone with a partner who not only had worked a very slow patrol station, but he actually admitted to being afraid of south central LA. He was fun to play with. I took him to every bad-ass place in FPK I could think of and for lunch I took him to a beat up little barbeque joint deep in the ghetto. There is *nothing* as good as real barbeque! But my partner wouldn't even get out of the car until I told him the owner was a retired cop and all the employees were pro law enforcement. Even with that, I don't think he enjoyed his lunch very much.

GETTING SHOT DOES NOT FEEL GOOD

John Hawksley (a former Firestone deputy), our sergeant, and I were in the Metro Bureau office one morning when a request was received from Headquarters Auto Theft Bureau for assistance on a case they were working. Someone had hijacked a tractor/trailer at gunpoint. The rig contained over $100,000 worth of color televisions. Auto theft needed someone to go to East LA to interview an informant who possibly had information concerning the suspect and the truck's location. We took the assignment and headed for an area of ELA known as the "Mexican Alps". It was a hilly area with narrow, winding roads, not far from the Sheriff's Academy.

Unfortunately, due to a shortage of detective vehicles, we were again using our own cars, and therefore had no department two-way radio. And, this was at a time before cell phones had been invented; so once we left the office we were without communications. In the fifteen or so minutes between leaving detective headquarters and arriving at the location, it became clear to those in the office that we might actually be going to something other than an informant's house. Unfortunately, we didn't know that, as there was no way for us to receive an update. It soon became apparent that something had changed.

The house we were going to was down in a little valley behind a "mom and pop" convenience store. John and I went down towards the house while the sergeant stayed up top. As we got to the front porch, the door flung open and within a second, a male with a gun stepped out. John and I went for our weapons, but John got shot in the chest, and as I went into the "FBI crouch" that we'd been taught at the academy, I was hit in the left arm. Bringing my left my arm up across my chest while I drew to fire with my right hand undoubtedly saved my life. Had my arm not been there to intercept it, the bullet would most likely have hit me in the heart. I thanked God then for saving my life, and I still thank Him today.

John and I both returned fire, but we were shooting hurt and shooting blind, as the subject had stepped back into the darkened house where we could not see him. In spite of being critically wounded, John grouped five rounds into a tight 3-inch circle in the door frame. My rounds killed a color television in the living room. Using the phone in the convenience store, our sergeant, after firing a couple of rounds himself, got plenty of help coming from ELA Station. The shooter was eventually detained, and John and I were transported to hospitals. Due to his critical injuries (from which he eventually recovered fully), John was sent to LA County General Hospital's trauma center. I went to St. Francis.

TAKING CARE OF EACH OTHER

On the way to the hospital, I was asked who I wanted to notify my wife. I asked that Deputy Tim Birkeland, a former partner of mine at FPK and now a firearms instructor at the Academy, make the notification. Firestone Station was also notified, since the Department knew I still lived in FPK's area. Firestone is like the Marine Corps. Once a FPK deputy, always an FPK deputy so, without being asked, they sent personnel to notify Patty as well. And, because Firestone always thinks ahead and plans well, they sent a female deputy to watch our children so my wife could be brought to the hospital. The deputy watched the kids until Patty's mom and sister arrived to take over.

This incident prompted some changes in how the Detective Division did business. While there would never be enough radio-equipped county vehicles to go around, the Department freed up some old, but still usable, two-way radios, and allowed us to install them in the personal vehicles we used on duty. When my arm healed to the point where I could do it, I spent a lot of time installing those radios in detectives' cars. Mine was the first. Today, forty years later, I serve as a reserve deputy sheriff in the small, rural county in which I live. I have a personally-owned public safety radio in my own pickup. Some lessons are never forgotten.

Light Duty

The next nine months saw me go through three surgeries to reconstruct my arm. After one month of being off work, I was stir crazy and driving my wife nuts, so I requested to come back to work on light duty. The Detective Division chief approved my request, and I was assigned to the Headquarters Detectives watch commander's desk.

That was a busy time for Headquarters Detectives. We were still providing around the clock witness protection in Firestone, acting as security for the Black Panther trial in Superior Court, and assisting with the on-going Charles Manson investigation. Plus, we suffered the tragic loss of two detectives who were gunned down in the line of duty. As the duty officer at the watch commander's desk, I often found myself briefing the Division Chief or even the Sheriff himself on major developments in on-going cases. Sitting at the desk, however, was not really my ideal activity.

At one point, the Commander of Intelligence Bureau asked if I was willing to try to get some intelligence info from the Manson "family" members who were camped out in their own van next to the Hall of Justice during Charlie Manson's trial. The thought was that with my beard, mustache, and long hair, plus with my arm being in a cast, the "Manson girls" wouldn't make me for a cop. As it offered an opportunity for occasional relief from riding a desk, I enthusiastically agreed.

While Charlie and others were already on trial for the infamous Tate-La Bianca murders, there were other murders and many other crimes that were unsolved and that the Manson Family was suspected of committing. Just being able to listen in on what Manson Family members like Sandy Goode and Lynette "Squeaky" Fromme were talking about was thought to be a good source of intelligence information.

So I began to hang out with the Manson girls from time to time, and for some reason they accepted my presence and of course never imagined I was a cop. Information obtained led, at one point, to the arrest of the aforementioned female Charlie followers for possession of sawed-off shotguns. Later information led to the capture of Warren Marchelette and Kenneth Como, two Manson family members who escaped from the 13th floor of the Hall of Justice Jail by rappelling down the side of the building on bed sheets.

MEETING MANSON

LASD was still investigating Charles Manson well after his arrest in the Tate-La Bianca murders. He was an evil that simply wouldn't go away, nor would his many followers who were suspected of involvement in many of the crimes which LAPD and LASD thought Charlie had committed, but hadn't yet been proven. There were some bodies yet to be found, and for that reason, whenever the Manson girls took off on a jaunt to some place like the Mojave Desert, they were followed.

One day, both Homicide and Intelligence Detectives wanted to interview Manson again, to see if he might implicate himself in additional crimes. I was asked to sit in just to see if anything he might say might connect with anything I had heard the Manson girls say.

Charlie was housed in the Hall of Justice Jail because he was on trial for the Tate-Law Bianca murders, and the trial took place in the same building. I accompanied the other detectives to an interview room, and several jail deputies brought Manson into the room. There are no details I can share about what Manson said because it was all nearly incoherent gibberish. Every time he was asked a question, he launched into some weird conversation that did not relate to anything he was asked.

I will say this, however: I have never in my life felt uncomfortable in anyone's presence…except Manson's. When I looked into his eyes, it felt like I was looking at the devil. His eyes were piercing and wild – that's the best I can describe them. I mentioned that later to the other two detectives, and they assured me I was not the only one to feel a little chill go down my spine when in Manson's presence.

GIVE 'EM HELL, PETE

On two occasions, I was assigned to Sheriff Pitchess' security team. He normally wouldn't have such a team (just a driver), but he was recuperating from open heart surgery, and he and his family, as well as the judge trying the Manson case, had received death threats. Pitchess was a powerful political figure; some considered him to be the most powerful politician in California at the time. As mentioned elsewhere, he was on a first-name basis with President Richard Nixon.

The highlight of my time on his security detail was at a large fundraising dinner he attended at the Beverly Hilton hotel. The keynote speaker was the very liberal and arrogant Senator Ted Kennedy. This was after his brother, US Attorney General Robert Kennedy, had been shot and killed by Sirhan Sirhan at the Ambassador Hotel in Los Angeles. Pitchess had outlined a security plan for Ted Kennedy designed to insure that Ted would not become another victim.

Right after the dinner and just before the keynote address, everybody at the head table took a break and came backstage to where our security team was stationed. Pitchess walked up to us and asked our sergeant if Kennedy was following the security precautions. Our sergeant answered honestly: no, Senator Kennedy was not following instructions.

Pitchess walked up to Kennedy in front of numerous Hollywood Stars, poked Kennedy in the chest, and yelled at him, "You son of a bitch, I'll be damned if I want another Kennedy shot in LA County. You do what my security people tell you. Do you understand?"

Kennedy's only response was, "Okay, Pete, I'm sorry."

For the duration of the event we had no problems with the Senator.

GOD HAD A PLAN

Nine months after being shot, I was cleared to return to full duty and was looking forward to going back on the streets full time as a Metro detective. The day before I was scheduled to do so, Inspector Paul Bratsch, who was second in command to the Division Chief, called me into his office. He told me that Division headquarters was getting so busy that they had decided he needed an aide. He offered me the position. I started to decline, since I really wanted back in the action. He interrupted me and said that on slow days I could go in the field with Metro, but by working for him I'd have Monday through Friday 8am to 4pm hours. He suggested that in the evening I could go to grad school. I took the offer.

About a month later, the sergeant who was aide to the Division Chief had to retire on short notice for medical reasons. Chief Ray Holt called me into his office and told (not asked, but told) me I was going to be his new aide. I would be an acting sergeant (no stripes, no sergeant's pay). I was on the sergeant's promotional list at the time, but everyone's best guess was my promotion wouldn't occur for four months. The Chief's proposition was simple: I would work as his aide until my promotion came up, and then he would guarantee that I would go to patrol as a sergeant, rather than to the jail. In the meantime, I could continue my evening grad school classes. I couldn't pass it up.

About four months later, I was promoted to sergeant. Chief Holt tried to get me transferred to Firestone, but they had no sergeant's vacancies. I went to Norwalk Station patrol. It was the worst assignment of my LASD career, except for getting to work with some former FPK partners who were Norwalk sergeants also. Fortunately, my time at Norwalk would be limited.

Chapter XIV:

The Beginning of the End

I disliked Norwalk from the start, due mostly to the captain who ran it. He was not my type of cop. I looked at the assignment as purgatory.

I had been at Norwalk for maybe two months when the Sheriff announced that a new substation was going to be built in the City of Carson. That station was needed because Carson was growing rapidly. The plan was for the new station to take over policing responsibility for Carson from Firestone. In addition, Firestone would lose the unincorporated East Torrance, Keystone, Dominguez, and East Compton patrol areas. Firestone would be left with the North End and Willowbrook proper. That was the beginning of the end for Firestone, though its total demise would take nearly another twenty years.

The unique thing about Carson Station was that the captain would get to pick his own crew. All lieutenants, sergeants, and deputies would be those selected by Captain Logue. You could apply, and a lot of folks at all ranks did. But only those Logue wanted were chosen.

The new station was set to open in November of 1974. In July, those selected would be notified and the lieutenants and sergeants would actually leave their current assignments and work at the under-construction Carson station trying to get everything ready for opening day.

GETTING OUT OF PURGATORY

One Norwalk lieutenant and three Norwalk sergeants were selected for transfer to Carson; I was one of the sergeants. All of us had worked Firestone in the past, so we knew the new station's area quite well. As it developed, we also knew most of the deputies who would be assigned to Carson, since we had worked with almost all of them at FPK.

Once we had re-located to the under-construction station, we were tapped to assist Firestone on a number of occasions. When they needed coverage, several of us sergeants were "loaned" to FPK for a day or two at a time to work as patrol sergeants. So while I was never officially assigned to Firestone as a sergeant, I did work as 10-Sam and 15-Sam (sergeant's units) on more than one occasion.

THE FIRST SHIFT

The night Carson opened was the night Firestone started to die. I worked the first shift as a Carson patrol sergeant with Lieutenant Jay Wickler riding along with me. Unit 160-Sam-Lincoln made the first legitimate felony arrest out of Carson station. Fifteen minutes after midnight, fifteen minutes after Carson Station became "official", Jay and I arrested a suspect for "rape in progress". It was not the result of a call, but an observation. We were patrolling a closed industrial area with lights out when we came across an occupied vehicle. A female who had been kidnapped at gun point was being raped by an ex-con on parole. That was not only Carson's first felony arrest, but a very satisfying one.

WHAT?! IT'S NOT FOR US?!

I will share a couple of Carson (formerly Firestone) stories, just because I can.

A few days before the station opened, they were bringing in furniture and supplies in big trucks. Carson was a big and very modern station. It included things no other station had....like a workout room, break room, and sleeping quarters for deputies who might get off duty at 3am and have to be in court at 8am. As they unloaded one of the trucks, we noticed a nice big color television, weight machine, exercise bike, pool tables, and tons of stuff that we thought were headed to the deputies' workout and break rooms. Another sergeant and I commented that it was really nice the Department was finally taking care of the troops. The Utility deputy who was supervising the delivery laughed.

"This isn't for us, it's for the inmates", he told us.

The county's "Inmate Welfare Fund" had purchased all of that equipment for use by station trustees (inmates) who performed work (janitorial, etc.) around the station in exchange for reduced sentences. We were just a bit disappointed.

HORSING AROUND

The second story deals with a prank I played on one of my favorite lieutenants, which just about backfired. It may explain why I don't play pranks very often. As I mentioned earlier, my-father-in-law was a transplanted Midwest farmer who kept horses at a place the family owned on the Mojave Desert. Through his influence, I actually became a horseman of sorts, and that carries over to today. On the small ranch where we now live, I've bred, raised, and trained both American quarter horses and American paint horses, and I ride on a regular basis.

One graveyard shift, I was working as the watch sergeant inside the station. We were short on sergeants, and were actually running without one in the field. About 3am, I heard one of the units dispatched to a call about three blocks from the station. It involved two stray Shetland ponies that were walking down the middle of Carson Boulevard. The two-man unit arrived and confirmed that, indeed, there were two such animals that must have escaped from the backyard pasture of a house in the neighborhood. The deputies asked what they were supposed to do. I had an idea.

I told the dispatcher to advise them I would be en route. I had the watch deputy cover my desk, and I took the sergeant's unit and drove to the scene. I knew we kept some rope in the trunk of that vehicle. When I got there, I fashioned two rope halters and put them on the ponies. I told one of the deputies to drive my car back to the station, and that I would walk the ponies there and tie them to the station flagpole. Either the owner would call when he found them missing, or Animal Control could come and get them later in the morning when they were open for business.

On the way back to the station, I had one of those "the devil made me do it" moments. When I got the ponies to the station, I tied them to the flagpole and went inside. I asked the watch deputy where the lieutenant was, even though I was pretty sure he was in the break room having coffee and reading the paper – which is where he usually was when things were slow. I hatched my plan.

I would walk both ponies up the ramp from the parking lot, through the outside door, and into the booking cage which, at the time, was devoid of any prisoners. I had the jailer poised ready with a Polaroid camera. Once the ponies were in the cage and the camera ready, we would hit the jail panic alarm, which sounded throughout the station. I knew that would bring the lieutenant running up the stairs from the break room, huffing and puffing, to see what was going on. I told the jailer to get a photo of the look on the lieutenant's face when he saw not a fight in the booking room, but two ponies instead.

Everyone was ready, the panic alarm was hit, and shortly thereafter we could hear the lieutenant running up the stairs, keys jangling. Rather than glance at the glass-windowed booking cage, the lieutenant kept running, head down, around to the side door of the booking cage. He thrust his jail key into the lock, opened the door, stepped in, and promptly slipped on some freshly dropped horse poop. That caused him to fall on his butt and slide under the ass end of a pony, and left him looking up at the four-legged creature. It was precisely at that point that the jailer took a picture of the lieutenant's face - and about 100 milliseconds before the Lieutenant screamed, "Boyd I'm gonna kill you, you son of a bitch!"

After a few minutes, a shower, and a uniform change, the lieutenant actually began to see the humor of the stunt we had just pulled, and actually began to laugh about it. He even thought it was funny when his picture, in a plain envelope, was mysteriously slipped under the door of the captain's office.

SAVED BY AN RTO (DISPATCHER) – AGAIN!

One night, just a week prior to the opening of Carson Station, I was "loaned" to Firestone as a sergeant, and I responded to cover a deputy in the south end who was handling a disturbance call. One of the goals when handling such calls is to diffuse the situation and to calm down the participants. This is key to avoiding that huge Firestone "no-no" called "return and handle to conclusion".

I had not worked with this deputy before, though I would do so in the future as he was going to Carson once the station opened. I had heard that he had a "short fuse", and from time to time would agitate people unnecessarily. His reputation did not fail him on this particular call. As we left, I was all but certain we, or someone, would be back later to "handle to conclusion".

I have never viewed the role of a good sergeant as micro-managing or nit-picking. I did believe the sergeant's role was to provide advice when warranted, and sometimes to provide correction. Both advice and correction were needed in this instance. So, as we left the location, I requested that the deputy meet me at a closed gas station a couple of blocks away.

As mentioned before, in this era, LASD personnel, regardless of rank, did not have handheld portable radios as cops do today. However, that had just changed, and sergeants, including me, had only recently been issued a handheld radio which was actually what was called an extender. Worn on the belt with a microphone on a cord, you could receive the radio room's transmissions when out of the car. When you transmitted with an extender, it actually keyed the transmitter in the radio car to talk back to the radio room. Neat device…when it worked right.

I got out of my car to talk to the deputy and suffice it to say he was *not* in the mood for either advice or correction. Though he eventually apologized, which saved him from discipline for gross insubordination, he unleashed a tirade of profanity concerning how he was always being second guessed…yadda, yadda.

Sergeants are expected to maintain their composure when dealing with argumentative subordinates. But this guy was over the top. The only way to get his attention and get him to listen was to out-shout him and match him in profanity. That is precisely what I did. As I said, ultimately he apologized and got the point I needed to make.

As I got back in my car after having some meaningful dialog with the deputy, I was greeted by the not-so-warm glow of the red transmit light displaying on the Motorola radio in my unit. That was not a good sign, as it meant the car radio was transmitting. I depressed the push-to-talk switch on the radio microphone itself, and when I released it, the red transmit light was still on. I did the same thing to the microphone button on my extende,r and the red light remained on. I was sweating now, because if that transmitter was on the whole time the deputy and I were yelling profanities, it was likely that all of it got broadcast to the world – or at least to a meaningful part of the world, like LASD and FPK.

In something of a mild panic, I turned off the extender on my belt and immediately the red transmit light went off. Uh oh. I could be in trouble. About that time, over the radio, the RTO said (with just a hint of a laugh in her otherwise professional radio voice), "10-Sam, 10-21 the radio room" (that was a request for me to call). The closed gas station had a pay phone, and I wasted no time calling the RTO.

She seemed to take a great deal of satisfaction in telling me that she had heard 100% of the exchange between the deputy and me…but realizing what was happening, she shut off the repeater about five seconds into the exchange so that no one other than she heard it. In short, she saved my butt.

RTO's were considered our angels because their attentiveness and dedication was known to save lives. This may have been an unusual lifesaving, but it was one nevertheless. En route to work the next day, I made a major detour to the radio room in the basement of the Hall of Justice with a box of fine chocolates in hand.

CHANGE OF TACTICS

Not long after I was promoted to sergeant, the Department instituted a program called APSET (Advanced Patrol Special Enforcement Training). It was initially geared for deputies, and was taught by members of the Department's Special Enforcement Bureau (SEB). The idea behind the program was to contribute to officer safety by teaching tactics similar to those used by SWAT, but more importantly to give field deputies a better understanding of what SWAT could do, and when to request a SWAT response. Advanced crowd and riot control training was included, along with a little touch of mountain rescue training provided by the Emergency Services Detail (ESD) thrown in just for drill.

SEB, being SEB, threw a few "confidence builders" into the training, like teaching deputies to rappel off buildings and to chimney-climb rocks to great heights. Make no mistake, it was excellent training. APSET was well received, and at some point it was decided to extend it to sergeants.

Somehow, I was assigned to the first sergeants only APSET course, and it was outstanding training. Upon completion of the course, the sergeants were told that in a major policing incident we might be used as squad leaders for deputies who had also received the training. That actually happened at the Rose Parade one year when Sergeants Denny Curran, Glenn Thompson, and I (all APSET-trained) led squads into Pasadena City College to clear out rioters. But that's a story for another time.

I recall responding, as a sergeant, to a burglary-in-progress at a commercial building in Firestone's area during one of those times I served as a Firestone field sergeant while awaiting the opening of Carson Station. Deputies had arrived and had seen a suspect inside an office building. Prior to APSET training, they (and I) probably would have opted to make entry to capture the suspect. One of the benefits of APSET was that it helped us recall that SWAT existed for calls precisely like that one. So as much as we wanted to arrest the suspect ourselves, we opted for a better and safer tactic: the use of SWAT. While doing so made sense, it was a real transition from the way Firestone had done things in the past.

CENTURY STATION

In the years to come the Cities of Lynwood and Compton, which bordered what remained of Firestone's area, decided to give up their own police departments and contract with the Sheriff's Department for law enforcement. It made sense to have one geographically centralized Sheriff's station large enough to serve the North End, Willowbrook, Compton, Lynwood and unincorporated areas like East Compton. Thus, Century Station was opened, and in 1993 Firestone would close its doors forever.

While Firestone Station has closed, Firestone as an institution and as a style of policing lives on. There's a saying that as long as there is one surviving person who ever worked there, FPK will never die.

Chapter XV:
Conclusion

Carson was a good assignment. We inherited enough of Firestone's former territory to be pretty busy with a good dose of hot calls thrown in to keep us sharp. Even though my friend Sergeant Glenn Thompson and I always worked the same shift so we could carpool from south Orange County, the drive was getting old. My sons were growing older, and I still didn't have much time to spend with them. Plus, my wife was beginning to have some health issues which would later claim her life at the age of 40.

In addition to those considerations, there were some things going on in the Department that, at least for me, raised red flags. I believe in professional law enforcement which treats people fairly and objectively. But I believed then and I believe now that our job *is* law enforcement. Some of the feel-good social programs that may be politically correct can be done by anyone. They don't take a dedicated, trained cop, and in fact to commit cops to the feel-good stuff is a disservice to society. Cops need to deal with serious and violent criminals, and devote all their efforts to taking dirtbags off the streets.

As early as 1974, I sensed within LASD a de-emphasis on crime fighting, and an increasing focus on trying to keep everybody happy. Good police work does not lead to everybody being happy. LASD and other agencies began to align themselves with folks that were very much anti-law enforcement, acting on the theory that by befriending them, we could change them. I called BS on that then, and I do now.

In short, I became disillusioned with where the Department seemed to be headed. I knew that with my policing philosophy, even if I were able to promote to lieutenant or captain, I would have little or no impact on the Department's philosophy and practice.

In early 1975, the City of Irvine, California – a city in south Orange County just a mile from where I lived – announced that it was going to create its own police department. They announced a recruitment effort for three lieutenant positions. I applied and was selected to serve as the lieutenant in command of Area I, the entire southern portion of the 38-square-mile city, and home to the University of California, Irvine. After serving for three years as a lieutenant, I was promoted to captain and assigned as Operations Division Commander. During my time with Irvine, I managed to finally complete my Master's degree in Criminal Justice Administration. I also authored my first book and began teaching at both the Orange County Peace Officers Academy and Western State University College of Law.

In early 1981, the City of Coronado (San Diego County), recruited for Police Chief, and again I was fortunate to be selected. I served as that City's Chief for ten years. On May 13, 1985 (our 18th wedding anniversary), Patty died unexpectedly from heart failure brought on by the asthma she had suffered with for years. She was truly a saint, and how well my three sons have done in their lives is due largely to her influence.

By 1991, I had done all one can do in a relatively tranquil peninsula city like Coronado. It was time to move on. That year I was hired as Chief of Police in Martinez, California, the county seat of Contra Costa County, east of the San Francisco Bay area.

Five years later, the long term effects of the gunshot wound I suffered in ELA caught up with me, and I was forced to retire from full time law enforcement. While at Martinez, I met and married my wife Jay; a year later, our beautiful daughter Ruthie was born (and is now entering young adulthood). We have since "retired" to a rural county in the Pacific Northwest, where I still serve as a reserve Sheriff's deputy when I'm not working with horses.

I've enjoyed a long and satisfying career in law enforcement. It began at Firestone, and the lessons learned at FPK influenced my decision-making for decades thereafter. I was honored and privileged to work with the fine folks of FPK. To them I will always be grateful.

REMEMBERING

In the history of Firestone Station, many deputies were either killed or injured in the line of duty. All of them deserve our thanks and prayers for their service. In these pages, I want to pay tribute to some of them. Each of the ones listed were deputies I worked with. Their loss had a great impact on all of us.

On December 8, 1970, Deputies Lou Wallace and Al Campbell stopped a suspicious suspect in Willowbrook during the early hours of the morning. While the suspect was being searched, he pulled a .32 caliber handgun, fatally shot Lou, and wounded Al. Before succumbing to his wounds, Deputy Wallace fatally shot the suspect.

On May 5, 1971, Deputy Gary Saunders went in foot pursuit of a suspect in the Florence District of Firestone's North End. At the conclusion of the chase, the suspect was able to overpower Deputy Saunders, take his revolver, and execute him.

Later in 1971, Deputy Ken Weiland was shot and critically wounded on the parking lot of Harbor General Hospital. If the incident had occurred anywhere but 100 feet from the emergency room, Kenny would likely have died. He retired as a result of his injuries.

On April 19, 1979, Deputies George Barthel and Jim Hollingsworth stopped a group of suspects in the Nickerson Gardens Housing Project. Suspects opened fire, killing George, and wounding Jim.

On March 19, 1983, Deputy Larry Lavieri was shot and killed after responding to a suspicious suspect at a gas station call.

These were all fine deputies***May they rest in peace

Made in the USA
Charleston, SC
12 December 2011